Dedication

This book is dedicated to the psychological pioneers who developed the theories of CBT, DBT and Positive Psychology. Their work has provided the foundation for this book. It is also dedicated to the practitioners and students of psycho-social education who share my conviction that practical, psycho-educational learning is essential for effective Counseling and Mental Health. Clinicians who incorporate life skills training into their practice realize that, as therapists, they are uniquely positioned to offer life skills to their clients, and thereby help them to make immediate and meaningful changes. With the conviction that life skills are essential to success in both professional and personal life, mental health professionals with a psycho-educational focus can serve as catalysts for long lasting life changes. This book is dedicated to the growing numbers of mental health practitioners who promote psycho-social education in their work, and who provide their clients with new life tools and skills to help them manage challenges throughout their lifetime.

ENDORSEMENTS

"*127 TIPS* delivers a wealth of ideas, skills, and exercises to apply and customize to a vast array of clinical issues and situations. Speaking to eclectic and integrative therapists (who comprise the majority of working practitioners), Judith Belmont taps in-demand and evidence-based treatments for their most practical interventions and teachings. Filled with psychoeducation, handouts, and worksheets for clients, active therapists will find TIPS to be a frequent and effective resource."

Lane Pederson, PsyD, author of *The Expanded Dialectical Behavior Therapy Skills Training Manual* and *DBT Skills Training for Integrated Dual Disorder Treatment Settings*

ABOUT THE BOOK

For your convenience, we have established a dedicated website to download all the worksheets and exercise from this book. This gives you a choice to photocopy from the book or printing the pages. The exercise will be labeled with the corresponding titles and pages.

go.pesi.com/127TIPS

ACKNOWLEDGEMENTS

Since the release of the first two books in the *TIPS and TOOLS for the Therapeutic Toolbox* series, I have been delighted to see the increasing interest mental health providers have in using practical, psycho-educational resources in their work with clients. This enthusiastic response has led me to write this third book with more TIPS and TOOLS, which includes recent technological and social media strategies. This book would not have been possible without insights I have gained through working with my clients who demonstrated the positive impact of various "hands on" strategies and interventions.

I am very thankful for the very competent team at PESI for being so supportive and encouraging in the entire process of developing this book, as well my previous books with them. Publisher Michael Olson, Business Manager and Publisher, Linda Jackson, Editor Kayla Omtvedt, and Cover and Layout Designers Amy Rubenzer and Matt Pabich have ensured the high quality of this book. Their integrity and professionalism is much appreciated.

Of course, the support from my family has also been invaluable, especially from my husband, Don, who has encouraged and supported me every step along the way.

If you would like your tip to be included in my next book in this series, please email your tip to: *judy@belmontwellness.com*

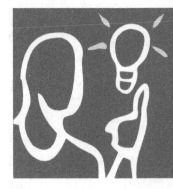

CONTENTS

CHAPTER 3: COGNITIVE BEHAVIOR THERAPY BASICS   41

CHAPTER 4: DIALECTICAL BEHAVIOR THERAPY (DBT) MADE EASY   65

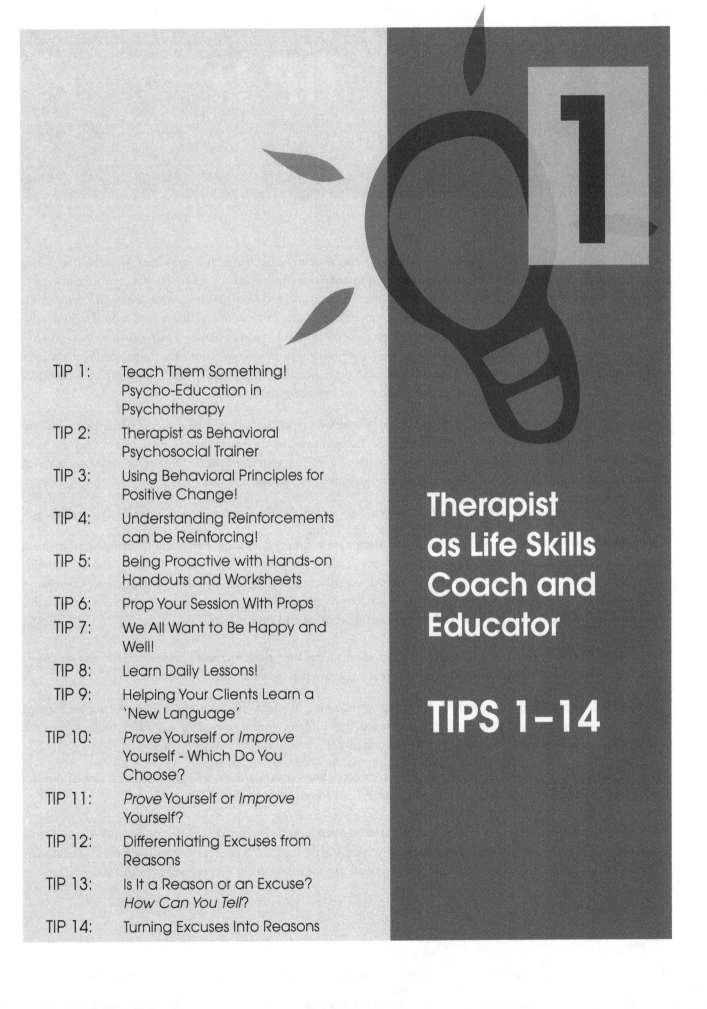

1

Therapist as Life Skills Coach and Educator

TIPS 1–14

TIP #1

Teach Them Something!
Psycho-Education in Psychotherapy

THEORY: Most mental health professionals and their clients work towards change, but knowing *how-to* facilitate change is often the dilemma. Even if it is obvious what our clients need to handle life better, the *how-to's* often remain elusive. This book follows my other two *TIPS and Tools* books by offering practical and effective tips to make lasting life changes. The practical focus of this series provides mental health professionals with an array of activities, mini-lessons, reproducible handouts and worksheets to help clients learn *how to* make changes. The workbook series offers tools to help you help your clients learn basic life skills that are, unfortunately, rarely taught in formal education. They are shared with the belief that practical life skills are essential to success in life, both professionally and personally, and that therapists are uniquely positioned to offer these skills and process them with clients in a meaningful way.

Some clients see counseling as something that *works* or *doesn't work*, and this book will help clients take a more active role in their treatment. This newest book in the *TIPS* series helps clients and therapists alike be proactive in the therapeutic process. Even for the most treatment-resistant client, these *TIPS* for your therapeutic toolbox can offer some much-needed new and refreshing help in addressing even longstanding and persistent issues.

As Confucius said so aptly, *"Teach me and I will forget, show me and I will remember, involve me and I will understand."*

This newest book of the series offers current ideas using new avenues for change. For example, using social media to support your clients and help them stay positive between sessions is a valuable addition to a more traditional counseling practice. At the same time, it also allows you to reach out to a larger audience. For those practitioners who want to widen their scope of influence – seeking to improve the lives of others with inspirational posts, books, ebooks, speaking, consulting, etc. – this book offers ideas of how to promote yourself and your message.

IMPLEMENTATION: These *TIPS and Tools* are designed to enhance the therapeutic experience in any setting by facilitating growth and healing through education, insight, active participation, and involvement.

The book follows the format of my other two books in the series, in which the *Therapeutic Ideas & Practical Strategies* are broken down further into *working TIPS* for each activity, handout, or general topic. Each *TIP* is broken down into *Theory, Implementation, and Processing*–hence the acronym *TIP*.

For some chapters, the worksheets and handouts for clients are self-explanatory, and thus the *TIP* breakdown and explanation introduces mainly the entire segment of the book, not each individual *TIP*.

PROCESSING: All the material in this book is meant to be reproduced for personal use with your own clients and group participants. The first chapter highlights some of my most widely used *TIPS* that fit well with almost any counseling model. They represent samples of universal themes that all therapists who focus on practical life skills will address.

TIP #2

Therapist as Behavioral Psychosocial Trainer

THEORY: Proactive therapists who offer psycho-educational tips, whether they know it or not, use behavioral principles in helping clients change. Even the widely adopted Cognitive Behavior Therapy model is based on the principles of behaviorism - *notice that the word behavior is even in the name!* Thus, understanding the cornerstones of behaviorism, i.e. *negative reinforcement*, *positive reinforcement*, *punishment* and *shaping*, can help the therapist apply these conditioning principles to help clients make positive life changes. In fact, in the *Dialectical Behavior Therapy (DBT)* model, founder Marsha Linehan writes of borrowing widely from behavioral principles to improve the psychosocial skills of DBT clients through activities designed to increase assertive communication. For example, *shaping* and behavioral practice offers DBT clients opportunities to improve their social interactions through role play and experiential activities to get valuable social skills practice.

IMPLEMENTATION: Since shaping and conditioning are at the foundation of psychosocial learning, a brief description of those terms will provide a foundation. The handouts in this book (starting off with TIP 3 and TIP 4) are based on behavioral principles and can provide insights into how behavioral principles can help actually facilitate awareness and change. Especially when we apply these insights into our own interpersonal attitudes and relationships, we collect a variety of tools in our toolbox to help alter unhealthy dynamics and facilitate change.

CBT and DBT inspired handouts provide a great springboard for group work, where individuals can help one another pinpoint both the healthy and unhealthy motivations that explain their behavior, and brainstorm what reinforcers they can use now to make positive changes.

Since relationships are so important to life satisfaction, I have included a whole section on Interpersonal Communication and Relationships later on in the book.

PROCESSING: Understanding the concepts of *positive* and *negative reinforcement*, *punishment* and *shaping* help to explain why social skills training, such as assertive training and use of role play, is so useful to help improve social skills for improving relationships. It also explains why some people *avoid* arguments at all costs (due to *negative reinforcement*) so as to avoid conflict (which is *punishment*). Learning new communication skills is then positively reinforcing! How can this differentiation help you and your client? The understanding of basic principles of behaviorism – a cornerstone of CBT, DBT and beyond – can add just another bit of insight to help clients understand what makes some behaviors hard to change, and focus on shaping their behavior towards more positive outcomes. The following resources will offer some insight and practice to differentiate between *positive reinforcement*, *negative reinforcement* and *punishment*.

TIP #3

Using Behavioral Principles for Positive Change!

Why do we act certain ways?

Why is it so hard to break old patterns even if we know better?

Why do we keep on staying in ruts even if we don't like it?

The principles of Behaviorism in the field of Psychology can offer insights into these age-old dilemmas: It's one thing to *want to* change – it's another thing t*o know how* to change!

This handout and accompanying worksheet can offer insights to some of the basic principles of Behavioral Psychology and show you how to apply them to your life to make changes NOW!

To start, we need to understand four important concepts of Behavioral Psychology: *positive reinforcement, negative reinforcement, punishment and shaping.* All these concepts apply to your actions and choices although you might not be aware of it!

Positive Reinforcement: A desired outcome that is reinforcing or rewarding in response to an action results in this action or behavior likely occurring again to gain further positive reinforcement.

Example: Working hard to do a good job so your boss will be happy, and you will be more likely to get a raise.

Negative Reinforcement: Refers to an increase in behavior to avoid or escape an undesired outcome.

Example: Exercising regularly in hopes of avoiding the need for medication for high blood pressure.

Punishment: A consequence that is aversive that is meant to decrease a behavior.

Example: Spanking or yelling at a child to decrease an undesired behavior.

Shaping: A gradual process to train or develop complex behavioral change by rewarding smaller parts or approximations that can lead up to the desired behavior.

Example: Training a dog to do a new trick and giving a biscuit on each small approximation of the overall goal.

Let's use a couple of examples for understanding and practice:

If we are training a dog to learn a trick, an example of *positive reinforcement* would be giving the dog food when the dog behaves in a way that is consistent with our goals for training. When a dog *stays* for even a moment, food is given, and after the dog *catches on* he would be expected to *stay* longer for the same amount of food. A dog that can *stay* for minutes at a time was initially reinforced to *stay* after only a few seconds, and increasingly the interval when the dog gets food is stretched. Thus, the behavior is *shaped*. It starts by reinforcing smaller actions to shape a more complex behavior i.e. *staying* or performing a trick.

Let's now apply to humans: Let's take a person who is shy and has a hard time speaking up and expressing herself. First, practicing in front of a mirror to rehearse what to say, and then practicing what you rehearsed in front of an encouraging and non-threatening family member or friend, would be an example of both *positive reinforcement* and *shaping*. Assertive skills improve with practice and once you are comfortable and build skills in non-threatening environments, the goal would be to feel more confident to assert yourself in a variety of situations. The end result – with behind-the-scenes practice – results in increased comfort in speaking up in a group, assertively confronting a co-worker who is rude to you, or asking for a raise. These behaviors often need to be shaped by reinforcing baby steps, such as asserting yourself with people you are more comfortable with before working on people that pose more of a challenge. As skills improve and you are reinforced by success of less threatening interactions, you can increasingly try to be more expressive with more intimidating situations. With practice, healthier behaviors are *shaped*.

Negative reinforcement might seem to have a negative connotation, but it is actually positive. *Negative reinforcement* is geared towards increasing a behavior to *avoid* or *escape* a negative consequence, or a *punishment*. We are often driven to avoid naturally occurring or social forms of punishment (such as being caught out in the rain without a raincoat or umbrella and being criticized or punished by a loved one). For example, take a couple who argues frequently and gets upset and angry with one another. The argument would be considered a *punishment*. Often, either one or both of the partners will avoid bringing up a sensitive subject to avoid a negative outcome, i.e. an argument. That would be *negative reinforcement*. They are reinforced by 'keeping the peace!' A partner might even go out of her way to try to ease their partner's stress, or avoid a blow up by enabling unhealthy behaviors just to avoid conflict (which could explain co-dependency)!

To avoid getting wet in our other example of being caught in the rain, especially after being "punished" by being caught out in the rain, you learn for next time to bring an umbrella with you in uncertain weather. Carrying an umbrella is an example of *negative reinforcement*. We use an umbrella to *avoid* getting wet. *Punishment* is when it rains and you do not have an umbrella. Often, after people are *punished* they learn behaviors to avoid being *punished* again. Taking an aspirin is an example of *negative reinforcement* – you want to escape a headache, and a headache is the punishment. Thus, *negative reinforcement* is not *negative* at all.

Why do these concepts matter so much in understanding our behavior and the behaviors of others?

By knowing these concepts, you not only develop insight but can use them to your advantage to make changes.

Avoiding getting close to someone? Perhaps in the past you might have had a wonderful marriage that was *positive reinforcing* that turned sour. After a tough break up (*punishment*) you are keeping people at a distance or having a hard time trusting so you won't get hurt again (*negative reinforcement*). Using the principle of *shaping* you might build trust again by spending more time meeting new people in social activities such as taking up a sport or taking a class, and getting to know someone of interest as a friend and develop trust slowly rather than rush into dating.

How about the case of alcoholism or drug abuse? You might argue that these would be examples of the unhealthy use of positive and negative reinforcement. That is because you are trying to feel good while escaping anxiety or depression by self-medicating to feel better temporarily. However, the effects of excessive alcohol or drug use can be quite punishing and can even lead to untimely death!

TIP #4

Understanding Reinforcements Can Be Reinforcing!

Using the handout, *Using Behavioral Principles for Positive Change (TIP 3),* identify examples from your own life of the 4 concepts.

Positive Reinforcement

_____

_____

Negative Reinforcement

_____

_____

Punishment

_____

_____

Shaping

_____

_____

Can you identify which are healthy and which are unhealthy patterns?

_____

_____

In the space below, write three behaviors or habits you would like to change. How can you use any of the four behavioral principles to achieve your goal?

1. _____

   _____

   _____

2. _____

   _____

   _____

3. _____

   _____

   _____

TIP #5

Being Proactive with Hands-on Handouts, Worksheets and Activities

THEORY: A *hands-on*, proactive approach helps clients develop new skills along with new insights, and worksheets and handouts provide invaluable skill building opportunities. What differentiates therapists from *good friends* is the expertise, insight, and ability to provide psycho-educational resources to educate clients to develop new strategies for thinking and behaving. Therapists who offer practical worksheets and handouts offer clients a valuable opportunity to learn and practice the *how-tos* for real change.

These skill building and informational materials lead to not only more rapid growth, but also to more longstanding change as new skills replace older ones. The therapist who can provide clients new life tools to manage life's stresses and challenges can offer skills to last a lifetime.

IMPLEMENTATION: This book is filled with handouts and worksheets to reinforce learning. I differentiate handouts from worksheets by referring to handouts as read-only written material to educate and inform, while worksheets provide clients the opportunity to fill in answers and process the information, personalizing their learning. To make more of an impact, a relevant *hands on* activity will further reinforce the concepts learned. Using all three modes of psycho-education (i.e. handouts, worksheets and an experiential activity) help clients make lifelong changes.

For example, CBT itself lends itself well to handouts and worksheets, and most CBT therapists have a repertoire of their own favorite handouts and worksheets, and in this book you will find many in the CBT section. I often make sure my clients have a short and to the point – often bulleted – informative worksheet, and then handouts to tailor their learning to their own situations that they fill out between sessions. I then structure an experiential activity to reinforce the writing and reading exercise. The more modalities of learning, the better. In this way, clients are engaged in various modalities to learn and experience the basic concepts of CBT and will likely incorporate new concepts better than they would have by just talking alone.

One example of a popular exercise from CBT that has been very effective with clients is a simple activity using a rubber band to help clients catch their negative self-talk. I give a rubber band to my client to use on their wrist to "snap" when they *should* on themselves or find themselves thinking irrationally. In the session, I help my client catch their *should* statements, whereupon they snap the rubber band on their wrist. I might even count for them the number of times I hear a *should* statement within a few minute period. Often, they are surprised at the number of *should* statements they make. You might follow up the activity by asking them to record how many times each day they snapped their rubber band on their wrist, even using a portable counter. The word *can't* is also a good word to catch!

Do you have a lot of your own favorite handouts that you created yourself? Those proactive therapists who have created their own materials over the years can self-publish a manual to offer to clients for a nominal fee to cover printing costs, or offer a pdf file for their clients to print themselves. I personally self-published a compilation of my favorite client psycho-educational materials at a local printer, *The Therapeutic Companion*, which accompanied my two previous TIP books. Clients buy my self-published manual for a minimal fee and this provides them with a basic handout supply as well as mini-lessons and activities for life skills learning. Especially for clinics, agencies, schools, and hospitals, consider compiling your own self-published manuals with your favorite handouts. This way, clients can have an organized compilation of the material to use during and in-between sessions.

PROCESSING: I have yet to find a client who did not appreciate having these "user-friendly" materials at their fingertips to reinforce the session's topic of discussion and therapy. They make their learning experiential and memorable. Many mental health practitioners, especially those who have been traditionally trained decades ago, underestimate their role of psycho-educator. A pro-active learning approach can offer your client new tools to look at old problems, and can reinforce new skills to last a lifetime.

TIP #6

Prop Your Session With Props

THEORY: Having visual props on hand to use as metaphors and analogies with clients is invaluable. So useful, in fact, that I reserved a whole section in this book for using metaphors in treatment. Using simple items from everyday life can serve as very powerful tools that evokes emotion and drives home your therapeutic message. As most therapists would agree, when a client "feels" something, the client is more likely to make changes. Metaphors evoke emotion and are memorable. Incredibly powerful metaphors are used so often in everyday life that we become immune to them as powerful agents of change and insight.

IMPLEMENTATION: In my office, I have some "props" that I use to demonstrate points with clients. For example, I use an eraser to make the point that mistakes are necessary to grow and learn. I use a bowling pin to represent assertive behavior. I urge my clients not to get "bowled over" by others, and remind them that even when the pin is knocked down it gets back up, standing tall! I use a crayon to help clients remember it is up to them to put color into their world, and not to see things in black and white! I use the finger trap carnival toy to demonstrate how people get stuck when they are in conflict, trying to prove that they are right. The more they pull, the more they try to be *right*, the more they get stuck!

I love using the image of a deck of cards, showing that even if the king and ace look the best, if you are playing Crazy 8s the lowly 8 is better. How about the really lowly 2 in Deuces Wild? *It ends up being the best card of the deck!* A deck of cards provide a great visualization to remind clients not to compare themselves to others. It's one thing to say it, it is another thing to *show* it and help them *visualize*. I also make the point that in the case of playing a card game, we play with the cards we are dealt. So even if you are dealt lousy cards in life, it is up to you to play them as best as you can, and you still might have a "winning hand" after all! An additional point I make using playing cards is that we need all kinds of cards to play a game, and we need all kinds of people in this world to make the world go 'round.

As you can imagine from these examples, props help unleash creativity in both the therapist and the client and they are fun to use too! In group settings, it is fun to brainstorm and share with one another favorite metaphors.

PROCESSING: Most clients love props, and it serves also to lighten up even the most serious session. As the saying goes, "a picture is worth a thousand words." To the right is a metaphorical *toolkit* my client made up after one of our sessions. She was very excited to bring it in and share it with me, and she keeps it on her kitchen counter with tags reminding her of important metaphors that help her to stay positive and keep calm while dealing with her three young children. Her metaphorical toolkit has provided great comfort to her during some stressful moments of motherhood. She has used her toolkit to teach her children life skills lessons. She is excited to have found a way to impart life skills to her children that she herself never learned until later in life, and by teaching them, it also helps her to stay focused!

TIP #7

We All Want to Be Happy and Well!

THEORY: Regardless of mental health discipline or training background, it is safe to say that we all share a common goal with our clients – we all want to be happy and live well. Even the most treatment-resistant clients, who sabotage their own success, still want to be happy underneath their resisting, rejecting or self-destructive behavior – that is why they are in treatment! Even if they are not in treatment voluntarily, I have yet to see a client who did not hold out for some hope that life would improve.

It is this fundamental desire for freedom to pursue happiness that is a right given even in the Declaration of Independence as our U.S. forefathers so aptly put, *"certain unalienable Rights, that among these are Life, Liberty and the pursuit of Happiness."*

Fun Fact: *One of the most popular courses at Harvard in the last decade was the class on Happiness, taught by Professor Tal Ben-Shahar, who offered students insights into studies on happiness and how to be happy themselves!*

The field of mental health is no longer mainly focused on mental disturbance, mood issues and pathology, but rather on how to *be and stay well* – how to *thrive* and not just *survive*. Especially with the emergence of positive psychology and increased research and attention to wellness, the focus on happiness and subjective well-being is central to the lives of many. Wellness in the workplace is also increasingly a focus for companies, wanting to keep their employees productive and happy.

As mental health practitioners, we have a responsibility to know and use resources for wellness. This focus has become more mainstream with the advent of the Positive Psychology movement, which dovetails very nicely with more traditional models of the counseling field, such a DBT and CBT. The focus on wellness is made much easier with the many resources available on the internet. Self-improvement and wellness have now intersected with mental health in a way like never before.

In a message from American Counseling Association's former President, Bradley Erford, in his President's message in the association's *Counseling Today* magazine, he emphasized the importance of making wellness a therapeutic priority.

IMPLEMENTATION: In this book, I have included not only a section on Positive Psychology but a section on using social media to promote your mental health and wellness message. For example, inspirational posts on Facebook and Pinterest are increasingly popular and provide a creative outlet for counselors to promote mental health topics such as forgiveness, overcoming regret, gratitude, and positive thinking. Through my own inspirational posts and focus on emotional wellness on social media sites, I personally have enjoyed spreading my mental health message to a worldwide community, and getting to know personally people from around the globe through comments, messages, and world-wide sharing groups of page owners. Through doing this, I have realized, *"It's a small world after all!"*

PROCESSING: Offering your client wellness and inspirational resources as an adjunct to therapy greatly increases their ability to improve their lives; they not only seem to get better quicker, but they seem to stay healthier and more positive. Look for more information about inspirational posts in the social media section.

One of the very positive outcomes of this intersection of wellness and mental health is that common human struggles concerning relationships, overcoming obstacles, healing and forgiveness are all more normalized. The stigma of mental illness and even seeking treatment is eased considerably. Even people with serious mental health issues find comfort in wellness blogs and posts since it addresses needs we all have and makes them feel less *different*. After all, in treatment as well as in the field of personal development and wellness, it's all about attitude, and offering people hope!

TIP #8

Learn Daily Lessons!

"What did you learn in school today?" is one of the most common questions asked by parents to their children every day after school. Yet many adults go through life without ever asking what they learned each day. Being mindful of learning daily lessons allows us to be open to change and growth. We often think of school as the place where people learn, but really life itself is the far more reaching school where we learn every day of our lives.

In fact, life is the greatest teacher of all – it teaches us things that no one else could.

Yes, some of life's lessons we would rather not have learned and some of what we learn we wish we did not have to – that is exactly what makes life such an excellent teacher. Life has its own natural and logical consequences. If life was predictable and always in our control, how would we learn? Things do not often go as planned, despite our best intentions. However, we can gain solace that we can learn and grow from what life teaches us, no matter what!

So ask yourself every day, "What have I learned?"

This simple question will help you:

- *Find lessons in everything you experience.*
- *Make the best out of things and grow from the most difficult of circumstances.*
- *Think of how you can make something positive come from a difficult lesson, even if this is one lesson you could do without learning!*
- *Make peace with the fact that sometimes you are on the "fast track" and other times you might feel more in the "remedial class" of life. We all learn at different rates.*
- *Focus on moving in a positive direction instead of measuring how far you "should have" come already.*
- *Make peace with the fact that sometimes lessons are learned the hard way.*

SUGGESTED ACTIVITY

Write down three things you learned today. For each item you write down, think of how you can use that lesson to improve yourself and your grip on your world. How can you use those lessons learned to improve your future? Think of one practical action you can take based on what you have learned.

Do you want to know how you can increase your odds that you will put your thoughts into action? Tell someone! Studies have shown that just by telling someone what you plan to do, you will be more likely to follow through!

> *"There is divine beauty in learning…To learn means to accept the postulate that life did not begin at my birth. Others have been here before me, and I walk in their footsteps."–Elie Wiesel*

TIP #9

Helping Your Clients Learn a 'New Language'

THEORY: As we all know, life can sting. People come to us with all sorts of hurts and challenges in their lives, seeking to heal but not knowing how to do it. There is no shortage of reasons and ways people feel broken, and besides support and having a safe place to "unload," they need new tools to move forward. When methods of coping no longer work, even if they had worked or at least seem to have worked in the past, the role of the therapist as the teacher of a 'new language' is vital for therapeutic success.

IMPLEMENTATION: Using the metaphor of learning a 'new language' with my clients has been helpful in opening doors that were stuck, and has offered hope to many discouraged by being stuck in old patterns. Everyone can relate to the concept that even if you pick up a new language relatively quickly, the first language is still very much ingrained in your habits of thinking and speaking. As we all know, foreigners who come to live in the US still have a distinctive foreign accent even after decades. Their first language is still their default.

I encourage my clients to consider that their emotional first language might have led them to faulty conclusions about themselves. They might still *carry the torch* and describe themselves in judgmental terms, keeping their *first language* as their *inner voice* from unhealthy parents and role models in their youth. Labels such as "lazy," "loser," "stupid," "selfish," and "fat" might be so much a part of the first language that it has hardened into perceived fact rather than pure fiction. As therapists, by educating our clients that the first language actually might be faulty (more like Pig-Latin!), we can give them a gift of hope that healing is possible if they learn a new, healthier language.

PROCESSING: The following are some pointers that might help in working with your clients.

- It might be useful to consider that their primary psychological language might have been quite faulty—as in the case of emotional, verbal or physical abuse.

- If they get impatient with their progress in therapy, reassure them that it is as if they learned *Pig Latin* for 18 years or more before coming to therapy. It's hard to break old habits of self-talk – that was your *inner voice* for so long! It will help clients be easier on themselves using this analogy.

- In exploring a new language, you are exposing them to a new culture, a new style of living, and this creates a tremendous opportunity to think flexibly and reinvent how they see themselves.

- This analogy can explain communication problems with family members, friends, and co-workers. Even though we *assume* people in our lives *should* understand us, and get frustrated when others misconstrue what we say, if we can accept that they just might be speaking another language, we will be less likely to anger!

- Learning a new emotional language gives clients hope in the aftermath of shattered dreams, relationship break-ups, and other causes of emotional derailment. The attitude of "Hey Self, I'm a work in progress–I'm learning a new language" can be quite comforting.

Seeing yourself as a therapist who is serving as a psychological and emotional translator, interpreter and language teacher rolled into one will help your clients heal and grow! The key point to reinforce is that no matter how difficult it has been for them learning languages in the past, anyone can learn a language if they keep practicing!

 Judith Belmont, MS (2013) • 127 More Amazing TIPS and TOOLS for the Therapeutic Toolbox: DBT, CBT and Beyond • www.belmontwellness.com •

TIP #10

Prove Yourself or Improve Yourself? Which Do You Choose?

THEORY: Why do people argue? They want to prove a point! What ends up happening? The point gets lost in the disagreement – because what the argument is about becomes less important than being *right*. That is why my clients often will not recall what *started it* or will admit to me that it was *"something so stupid."* The reason for the conflict then becomes so much less important to them than *proving* they are right!

IMPLEMENTATION: This distinction is a valuable one to use with your client during a session. For a self-help assignment, the following handout will reinforce this distinction. It can be a great guide for *getting to the bottom* of why your client needs to *prove* themselves. Some of the common reasons that people have a need to *prove* are deep seated insecurities, still wanting to prove themselves to a judgmental parent (even if the parent is no longer living but is *alive and well* in their heads), or wanting to feel better about themselves by being superior. Assure your clients that self-esteem never comes from these empty victories, but it comes instead by building themselves up by their own accomplishments and not at someone else's expense. After all, being right does not make them a better person!

PROCESSING: Hopefully, in the course of treatment our clients realize that proving that they are right is a short term victory at best, and erodes and even destroys a relationship at its worst. First of all, once an argument begins, it is very unlikely that the other person will admit you are right. *Proving yourself* will never work, as it entails being judgmental of *shoulds* to live up to – approval from others, as well as your own *inner critic*. It is not uncommon that my clients who frequently find themselves trying to *prove* something will eventually realize that they are not working on *improving* themselves. This worksheet is a great springboard for making the point that truly *improving* themselves results not from negativity and conflict but from positive actions and thoughts.

After all, being kind rather than being right wins in the end!

REMINDER TO MYSELF

INSTEAD OF TRYING **TO *PROVE* MYSELF,**

I WILL WORK ON ***IMPROVING* MYSELF!**

TIP #11

Prove Yourself or Improve Yourself?

One of the most common reasons for arguments is that people are *talking at* rather than *talking with* one another, trying to *prove a point* and be *right* while making the other person see how *wrong* they are. However, *proving yourself* will not help you *improve yourself!* It will end up eroding self-esteem, because proving yourself often arises from low self-esteem – it leads to empty victories. Additionally, relationships suffer because it ends up being a situation of *you* against *them*, rather than building the *we* in the relationship. Thus, when you are working on *improving* yourself rather than *proving* yourself, you are improving not only your own self-esteem but the relationship!

How about developing a motto for yourself using this distinction when you find yourself caught in trying to prove? One example is *"Don't Prove, Improve!"*

ASK YOURSELF!

If you find yourself needing to prove yourself, consider the following:

Reasons I want to prove myself:

_____

How can I alter my goals so I can improve myself?

_____

Is there a person or people from my past that were judgmental and critical, that were hard to please, and that could be triggering the current situation?

_____

What are at least two ideas that will help remind you to focus on *improving* rather than *proving*?

_____

If you focused on improving rather than proving, how would your life be different?

_____

TIP #12

Differentiating Excuses From Reasons

THEORY: In the course of treatment, I have been struck by how many clients feel disloyal when they recount hurtful memories or feelings about important people in their lives, past or present. Even if laced with a lot of anger, their invisible loyalties make them hesitant to "blame" or "complain." It is not uncommon for mental health professionals and clients alike to lump reasons and excuses together. However, there are important distinctions between them that can help you in dealing with your clients issues from the past as well as their current life predicaments.

IMPLEMENTATION: Educate your client about the distinction between reasons and excuses. In a nutshell, as your clients will see, looking for reasons is healthier than finding excuses, as excuses serve to pass the blame to things outside of themselves. Here are the main distinctions:

Reasons: Shed light and insight into past behaviors. The motivation is to become more enlightened and knowledgeable at no one's expense. Learning is the key!

Excuses: A defensive attempt to blame others and deflect responsibility. The motivation is to critique and judge others for your problems. Blaming is the result!

Have your client fill out the following worksheet in order to identify reasons from excuses, and to learn how to transform excuses into reasons. It is harder than it looks!

PROCESS: As you can see, the person who clings to excuses stays a *victim* and the individual who wants to find out reasons is more likely to have a *victor* mentality. Clients often are very sensitive to any intimation that they are playing the part of a victim, as that is certainly not their intention, and often cannot identify in themselves the defensiveness that is perpetuated by excuses. They can be reassured that by lowering their defensiveness, their need to blame and by replacing excuses with reasons, they end up feeling much more confident and empowered.

LOOK FOR REASONS NOT EXCUSES!

Excuses blame others and keep you a victim.

Reasons shed insight so you can learn from your experience.

Excuses make you a prisoner of your past, **BUT REASONS CAN SET YOU FREE!**

TIP #13

Is It a Reason or an Excuse? How Can You Tell?

Many people confuse reasons and excuses. They often feel guilty and disloyal for saying something about someone who caused hurt in their lives. However, if they do not address their thoughts and feelings, negative feelings will persist and limit their life in the present.

This is the difference:

Excuse: If you give an excuse, you are blaming people and other factors outside of yourself for your behavior, feelings or reactions. Excuses shift the blame and responsibility outside of yourself and you are then a victim.

Reasons: If you look for reasons, you are looking to shed light and understanding on the problem. Trying to understand why you feel the way you do and why you have reacted in certain ways is healthy and necessary to not be controlled by them anymore. There is nothing to feel guilty about if you are seeking to understand and shed light, without focusing on "faults." That is being responsible.

In times of stress, do you tend to make reasons or excuses?

For the following examples, decide if it is a <u>reason</u> or <u>excuse</u>. For each excuse, how would you change it into a reason?

Reason or Excuse

Example: __excuse__ I am insecure because I had a bad childhood.

1. _____ I am angry at him because he is always so critical!
2. _____ The relationship did not work partly because I was not able to tolerate the lack of respect he showed me.
3. _____ My ex cheated on me and that is why I now can't trust anyone.
4. _____ I have trouble trusting people after he cheated on me.
5. _____ I blew up because he would not stop yelling.
6. _____ I realize that I have a hard time dealing with criticism since my parents were critical when I was growing up. I developed an extreme fear of rejection and ridicule which I am working on changing now.

Your Turn: Can you think of an example of an *excuse* that you use in your life that you can transform into a *reason?*

1. _____ (excuse)

2. _____ (reason)

TIP #14

Turning Excuses Into Reasons

Use this example to differentiate a reason from an excuse.

Excuse: I lack confidence because my dad was very critical of me.

Reason: I have low self-confidence and I have irrational messages in my head that I keep on life support, many from when I was younger. I do not need to listen to them now. My dad was doing his best to raise me, but I need to separate myself from the message that I am not "good enough."

Thus, reasons give you something to work on, whereas excuses are just a "done deal."

Write examples of EXCUSES that keep you a victim.

_____

_____

Now transform your EXCUSES into REASONS. Ask yourself, *"How can I change the excuses to reasons so I will use victor and not victim thinking?"*

_____

_____

How would your life be different if you used more REASONS than EXCUSES?

_____

_____

When you focus on REASONS, you can focus on goals to manage the hurt and anger. When you focus on EXCUSES you stay stuck in a point of time and remain a prisoner of forces outside of your control!

2

Group Activities for Psycho-Social Education

TIPS 15–27

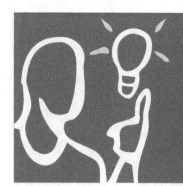

TIP #15

Personal and Collective Collages

THEORY: Creative and experiential group therapy sessions can offer fun opportunities for self-discovery in a social context. This activity that can be done individually but is ideal in a group setting and can serve both purposes of developing personal insight as well as providing a great forum for developing group cohesiveness and connection.

IMPLEMENTATION: Each person gets their own scissors, one or two heavy sheets of paper, with some glue to share for every few people. Have a supply of magazines and catalogs that contain colorful pictures. There are a few ways to do this activity:

- For a short activity, you can ask each person to find 5 - 10 words, phrases or pictures that describe themselves. They can glue the pictures onto one of their sheets and then members get to share their creative collage with the group.

- If you have more time, you might have group members use another sheet and have 5 or more words, phrases or pictures that depict how they would like to feel, how they would like to be, or what goals they have.

- A variation of using individualized sheets is having a poster board or flip chart for the whole group and have each person come up to the large group poster one by one, and put some of their own clips on the group poster. That way you create a group collage of goals, feelings, or interests and this further enhances group cohesiveness.

The instructions can be tailored to the type of group you have and the theme you want to address. For instance, in a drug and alcohol group, you might have two sheets - one being items that reflect what the destructive influences of drugs do and the other depicting pleasant images of things they enjoy in a drug-free life.

You can end the project either by having a time limit or by giving a set number of items on each collage. It is good to limit in some way since otherwise the project can seem to drag. More important than the clippings is the part in which everyone shares, so you would want to leave a lot of time for going around and having the participants share their creative collages (or talk about their contribution to the collective collage).

PROCESS: The feeling of universality and being comforted by the feeling that "I am not alone" is quite powerful with this exercise. It is a great introductory group project where members introduce themselves with the clippings as a springboard. Have them explain why they chose certain clips. Interestingly enough, some people choose more words and phrases, and others more pictures and metaphorical images. This is an especially good icebreaker exercise for children and teens that might feel more comfortable verbalizing to the group with the help of these colorful visuals. Since the sharing of tangible magazine clips is generally a non-threatening forum for self-disclosure, while providing a structured activity that allows for personal creativity, this is the type of activity that can be altered in a variety of ways for therapeutic as well as workplace wellness team building groups.

TIP #16

The Metaphoric Toolkit Activity

THEORY: Metaphors are very powerful agents of healing and change. Whenever I lead group presentations, I make sure I bring in plenty of objects to use that represent positive metaphors. Most of these objects are very small, inexpensive items that people can then take home to remind themselves of the metaphorical lessons to stay positive in their everyday life. They serve as tangible, visual reminders of the positive message of the group or presentation. People even months later have reported that they have kept the items in prominent places like on their desk at work, in their car, or on their kitchen counter to serve as reminders to stay more positive.

IMPLEMENTATION: I commonly have items and small plastic bags (which I buy inexpensively, sometimes in bulk online) arranged in a few compartmental displays, as shown below and have people assemble their own metaphorical toolkits based on the theme of group session or presentation. An example of metaphorical toolkit is in the next TIP, TIP #17, which I call *The Happiness Toolkit.* Clients or group participants are instructed to assemble their bags with items that represent to them ideas for staying positive, being happy, limiting stress, etc. If it is a relatively small group, I have them make up their bag during the session, and if it is a larger wellness presentation, I tell people to make up a kit when they arrive before the program starts to save time, and in the presentation give them about 5 minutes to share with the table their chosen objects.

Many times I also have my own toolkit already prepared, and I elicit responses from the group about what these objects represent. Brainstorming can be fun with a whole group. Another whole group variation is to have people take turns holding up one or two items that they chose, and share with the group the metaphorical meaning it suggests to them. For a team building activity, I might have small groups make up a group bag, and have each group share their items with the larger group. The variations are endless, depending on your purpose for the activity. Sometimes I have people take a few items from their purses or wallets that can serve as metaphors to share with the group. Following this TIP, I will have a sample sheet that you can distribute or keep in mind for yourself to help your group think in metaphors.

You might want to wait until the end of the session to do this activity, and have people go up during a break or towards the end, and ask everyone to take up to three items that will help them remember the main points that they got out of the session today.

Using a metaphorical toolkit is a great activity with groups of young children and teens!

PROCESSING: Whether I introduce this activity at the end or beginning of a program, across the board people have loved using items as metaphors and they have made my groups interactive, fun, and creative. The variations are endless of how you can incorporate metaphors into your group or presentation, and the important thing is that you process with the group to brainstorm ideas and tap into their creative juices! In the next TIP, I provide

a more detailed description of what can be in a metaphorical toolkit, in this case The Happiness Toolkit. TIP #17 will give you some creative ideas of how to use metaphorical objects which are all related to virtual ideas for a happier life. Other toolkit themes can be "The Drug-Free Life Toolkit for Addiction groups, The Relationship Toolkit (for reminders on healthy communication - which can be perfect for couples to make up together) or The Anger Management Toolkit (for Anger Management Groups). Another creative and effective idea for general therapy groups is to have one metaphorical object which represents the life skills topic for each group session, and by the end of (for example) a 12 session group, each member will bring home 12 items in the toolkit to represent each of the 12 session topics which can serve as reminders long after the group is over.

TIP #17

Make Your Own Happiness Toolkit!

The following are some ideas for making up your own Toolkit! They even make great birthday presents if you create your own kit and include a sampler sheet like this below explaining the symbolism of some common items.

Think of household items that can have metaphorical meaning while also having functionality.

With the help of a Happiness Toolkit, you'll have *happiness in the bag!*

These tools will serve as visual reminders to keep sane in your busy world!

Elastic/Rubber Band: Don't let yourself get stretched too thin – say "no" without feeling guilty and set limits. Also, elastic is like stress – we need some "stretch" to thrive. But don't stretch too much or you'll *snap!*

Crayon: Put color into your world – if you see things in black and white you will think in extreme and unhealthy ways.

Stress Ball: This is like a stress-resilient personality, as it bounces back, floats, rolls with the punches, is soft, flexible and maintains its shape no matter what.

Kaleidoscope: It always changes, transforms and is never stagnant. It offers the beauty of putting color into your world in all sorts of different ways.

Toy Fire Fighter: In your relationships, don't be the one to start fires, be the one to put them out! No matter how many fires someone else starts, you CAN stop it!

Pencil: Write your own destiny and write yourself a happy ending. It's up to you how your story turns out.

Eraser: It's okay to make mistakes – that's why we have erasers. You don't have to be perfect! Strive to be human, not perfect. Needing to be "right" is actually "wrong!"

Bubbles: You do not have to be a child to appreciate the importance of play in your life. Playfulness makes your life lighter and more free. Enjoy the floating feeling!

Deck of Cards: It's not the cards you are dealt, it is how you play the hand. Also, cards are like people – we need all types to play the game of life. At times, the lowly 2 is the best card, even though the King "seems" better. We need all 52! You can just include a card in a toolkit rather than a whole deck of course!

Magnifying Glass: Be a thought detective! One of the most important ingredients to happiness is to identify irrational and negative thoughts so you can change unhealthy thought habits!

Hershey Kisses: Spread the love! Keep one for yourself to remind you that self-love is necessary before you can love anyone else, and give the other away to someone as a Thanks! *Hugs* are good to include too!

Paper Clip: Hang onto positive people in your life!

Dice: Life is unpredictable – there is always an element of chance. You can't control the number you get; you play as you roll with it!

Timer: Schedule a time to relax, to have a mental vacation, to set time for yourself, and also schedule a worry time instead of carrying it through the day!

Bouncing Ball: You can bounce back from anything if you have a positive attitude and learn from the past! With this bouncing ball you can bounce higher than ever!

Finger Trap: Don't engage in conflict where you feel you must win over someone else. Strive for a win-win outcome. Otherwise, if you try to prove you are right, you get stuck in the trap!

Flexible Figure: Happiness and rigidity do not go together. Be flexible, be open to change and growth.

Marbles: In case you feel as if you are losing your marbles – here are some of mine to help you through!

Toy Soldier: Be strong and brave even if life does not go your way. Fight for what you believe in!

Sticky Note: Keep reminders or affirmations with you at all times to keep focused on your goals and remind yourself of positive thoughts that will help you through the day!

NOTE: You can also use larger metaphors for group demonstration purposes that are not for taking home, such as a large kitchen utensil or household object. An interesting variation to put some things in bags for small groups, who have fun brainstorming with their group what they can signify!

Can you think of more metaphorical objects on your own? Can you add a few more in the space below?

_____

_____

_____

_____

_____

THEORY: Balls are very versatile for group training. They provide opportunities for interaction, demonstration, experiential learning, and above all, FUN! From little bouncing balls to beach balls, balls can provide many quick and easy activities that are great in groups.

IMPLEMENTATION: The following highlights my favorite activities using balls of all sizes. These activities are by no means an exhaustive list of the versatility of using balls in group demonstrations and experiential activities. Rather, these are the ones I frequently use that I have found to be successful. Each activity can be quick and easily adapted to the seating arrangement of the group. If there is enough space to move around, everyone can participate. Otherwise, for a couple activities, I ask for volunteers to demonstrate. The key is to be flexible according to the situation and room set up, and just concentrate on "having a ball!"

1. Demonstration and Group Brainstorming: How is a Stress Ball Like the Stress Resilient Personality? Here are some common answers:

A Stress Ball:

- Floats (good demonstration)
- Flexible
- Bounces back
- Retains shape
- Soft
- Rolls with the punches
- No hard or sharp edges
- Safe, won't hurt you
- Colorful
- It's light (you might say it is a ball with a sense of humor!)
- It's also more fun when you play with someone else! (As I say that, I throw the ball unexpectedly at someone to *play catch!*)

Processing Question: "How would your life be different if you were resilient like a stress ball?"

2. Another stress ball activity was in a previous TIP book, and is repeated here since it is such a well-received activity, and a lot of fun! Invariably this activity brings on a lot of laughter!

Ask participants to stand and form circles of about five to eight people. Give each group one stress ball to begin. Have the first person throw a ball to someone else and remember who they threw it to since they will be asked to remember and continue the same pattern. If there is only one group, you can be part of the group, but if there is more than one, make sure you are not in the mix, since you will need to move around between groups. Each person throws the ball to someone who has not yet had the ball. The last person sends it back to the original person who "keeps the ball rolling" a little faster the next time. (Do not have them throw to the same person twice until all members have gotten it first.) Once they have the pattern down, introduce another ball – then another and then another. Balls drop, roll, etc., but urge them not to pick them up while you go around supplying other balls so as not to break the momentum of the group ball toss. With five or six balls going at a time for 5 or 6 people, it becomes quite a circus with a lot of laughing!

After people sit down, process the activity with the group. Point out how the most laughter was when the balls were coming fast and furious or when the balls dropped. Make the point that it demonstrates that making mistakes is not so bad! You might address how people deal with stress when they have a lot of "balls in the air," and what tips they relied on to keep focused in the activity. This exercise is also a great lead-in for the topic of mindfulness, noting that when they were engaged in the ball toss it is likely they were not focusing on what happened yesterday or wondering what they were having for dinner – they were too absorbed in the NOW. One other important point to make sure to note is that stress can be positive and fun as long as you manage it and not carry it!

3. Have a Beach Ball Toss!

Using a beach ball, start by throwing it to one person and ask the group to keep it up as it goes around the room with people seated – you might for fun and a big splash of color want to have few balls going in the room. The point to be made is that we need everyone to work together to keep the balls up – there are things we can't do alone. This is a quick and easy team building exercise, and sure to bring lots of smiles and active engagement!

4. Stress Is Like a Beach Ball!

Start with a beach ball inflated, deflate the ball and use this as a lesson to talk about stress. Stress is usually thought of as bad or negative but we need stress to be "full of life." Playing sports, watching your favorite sports team play, getting married, having a baby, going on vacation – it's all stressful but that is what makes life meaningful! It is convincing with the demonstration as you blow into the beach ball or a balloon and as it inflates it looks like it is supposed to with function and form, rather than being limp and lifeless. Of course, if you blow too much it looks like it will pop – especially with a balloon! Life is a balance of having enough stress to be vibrant and alive, not too much that you'll explode!

5. Catch – You're IT!

Using a beach ball or soft foam-type ball, ask a question relating to your current topic for the group, and throw the ball to someone to answer. After that person answers, then they ask a question on the same topic, and throw it to someone else to answer, and so on until the whole group got a turn. You might want to have another round with a different topic.

This is a great way to involve people, putting them on the spot in a fun way! In this exercise, even the quietest members of the group will likely be able to think on their feet and participate in between laughs!

PROCESSING: These sample ball activities bring some lightness and active sense of engagement to the group. There are many therapeutic takeaways—I offered only a handful. I personally had some foam stress balls personalized with my logo for my wellness speaking, and they provide great giveaways.

TIP #19

Good Questions for Groups

THEORY: Sometimes the quality of your group participation depends on the kind of questions you ask. Some seemingly simple questions can start a wave of sharing and camaraderie in the group, and require the individual to reach a part of themselves that they rarely visit as they reflect on thought-provoking questions. Asking good questions not only promotes healthy self-reflection – it helps build support and healthy self-disclosure.

IMPLEMENTATION: The following are some questions that are likely to elicit thought provoking responses and provide a great springboard for group cohesiveness and self-discovery.

You can either ask the entire group the same question and they go around and answer, or you can have notecards or strips of paper in a bowl and each person picks a question when it is their turn to read. You might even want to make copies of the following questions, and suggest to your clients that they ask themselves these questions every night.

GOOD QUESTIONS FOR GROUPS:

What was your first memory?

What is one of the most important lessons you learned in life?

What has been your greatest accomplishment?

What has been your greatest challenge?

What is the most important thing you hope for?

What was your dream when you were a child? How has the dream evolved?

What does your inner voice say? Is it a nurturer or a critic?

If you were an animal, what animal would you be?

Who is your best role model?

If you could change one thing from your past, what would it be?

How are you most alike and most different from your parents?

What well-known person in the news or entertainment are you most like?

What famous person do you most admire?

What person in your life do you most admire?

What is a question you want to ask the group?

PROCESSING: The feeling of universality is comforting for many, and that presents one of the greatest advantages of being in a group. These questions can certainly be asked in individual counseling, but the impact is much greater when shared and processed within a group setting as trust and camaraderie evolves.

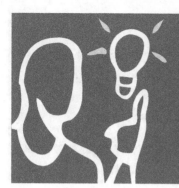

TIP #20

Do You Hear What I Hear?

THEORY: All too often we assume that people take our message the same way as we mean it. This exercise is a quick and fun exercise to do in a group and makes a very powerful point that you can't assume people hear things the way you mean them to be heard. We often perceive things differently than others realize. Don't assume they understand what you understand!

IMPLEMENTATION: Mike Iorio of Dale Carnegie Training in Pennsylvania originated this fabulous exercise for group learning. It's great for groups of all ages, as well as for wellness presentations and workplace trainings. It takes no more than 10 minutes for both the activity itself and the processing.

Ask for 5 or 6 volunteers to come up to the front of the room. (If you are running a small treatment group, everyone can participate.) Ask your demonstrators to stand before the room facing the people seated, give them a piece of paper (color does not matter, but various colored paper does make it more colorful!) and ask them to close their eyes and hold the paper out in front of them. Then give them specific instructions about what to do with the paper. The following is an example, but feel free to use your own variation. The exact directions are not as important as following the general format.

My directions: With eyes closed, hold the paper in front of you and fold the paper in half lengthwise. Then fold it over towards the floor, turn it 90 degree, rip off a little at the top left corner, then rotate180 degrees and take a very large piece off at the top left corner.

Then fold it again towards the ceiling and take a large piece off the top right corner.

Now open up your eyes and show us your unfolded paper.

It is really striking how just about everyone's paper looks like different snowflakes! They all heard the very same instructions, yet their interpretations and actions were very different!

PROCESSING: The point in this exercise is not to see if things are done correctly, but to show that so much of what we hear is a matter of interpretation. Almost everyone interpreted the instructions differently, resulting in different paper snowflake patterns. Too often people think that others understand them just as intended, but as in this exercise, it is clear that we all perceive things differently. This brings home the point that we need to clarify what people have heard us say rather than just assume they understand our message as we intended. No wonder why misunderstandings are so common!

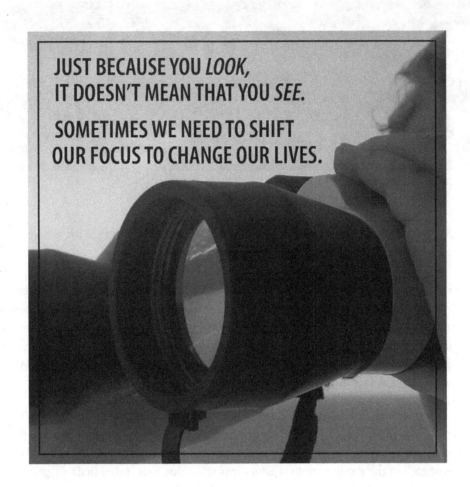

TIP #21
Turning Negatives Into Positives

THEORY: Structured group activities are powerful in reinforcing individual learning. This simple exercise will reinforce CBT principles of reframing and replacing negativity with positive thinking.

IMPLEMENTATION: First, introduce the CBT concept of reframing, which is basically a technique in which a negative thought is replaced by a more positive one by looking at it from a different "frame," or perspective. For a good visualization, you can actually demonstrate this concept by bringing in a couple very different looking picture frames with duplicates of the same picture in each, and discuss how the picture has a different look depending on the frame. Visualizations have a greater impact and are more memorable than merely talking about the concept in the abstract. After all, as the saying goes, a picture is worth a thousand words!

After the introduction to reframing, ask each group member to write down a negative thought they have about themselves or their lives that they would be willing to share with the group. When they are finished writing their answer, ask for a volunteer to read their negative self-talk to the group (make sure you instructed them to write a thought they would be willing to share). Then, each of the group members take turns reframing that individual's negative self-talk into a more positive self-statement. For example, if the first person states, *"I feel like I made so many mistakes in my life and I can't forgive myself,"* the next person could reframe it into a positive, such as *"You have had so many lessons in life to deepen you and make you wiser."*

When everyone has had a turn reframing the one thought, go back to the person who started this off and ask them to reframe their negative self-talk in their own words, after getting so many ideas from the other group members.

Go around the group until everyone has a turn. If there is time, you might have them actually draw two picture frames and put their negative self-talk in one and the positive reframing in another so they can bring it with them to reinforce the importance of reframing. Giving them a sheet with two picture frames to fill in makes the activity go especially well!

PROCESSING: This reframing activity is a great springboard for teaching and reinforcing the valuable life skill of being able to change a negative thought into a positive one. After all, *it's all in the way you frame it!*

TIP #22

Highlighting Positive and Negative Communication

THEORY: By observing the behavior of others and processing it as a group, we learn how to handle ourselves in a more assertive way. This activity helps highlight what makes people good communicators and what makes communication ineffective. After all, good communication skills are key to life happiness and success.

IMPLEMENTATION: Using notecards, I pass out one to each person and ask them to think of someone who has shown an example of positive and respectful communication. On the other side of the card, I ask them to write down an example of disrespectful communication that they have heard (without using specific names or identifying information to keep it anonymous). For example, during a presentation with nursing students on professional behavior, I asked for an example of positive communication at school or in the hospital practicum on one side of the card and negative or disrespectful conduct on the other. I then collected the cards so that the originator also remains anonymous (I tell them that this will be done beforehand so they will feel more free to use relevant examples). I then read aloud both sides of the cards randomly and this leads to great group discussions, likely because they are based on 'real life' situations.

PROCESSING: Taking the presentation for the nursing students as an example, each card I read prompted a lot of relevant responses from the others in the class. By taking their examples rather than making up my own, the students were very engaged as many of the issues raised were (of course) very relevant to them. The practical examples that remained anonymous were a great springboard for highlighting the elements of positive and negative communication. I always include a handout on assertive communication to refer to for this type of activity (See Chapter 7 for various communication handouts). Sprinkling a bit of role play in there always spices up the learning!

Here are some of their examples:

NEGATIVE, UNPROFESSIONAL CONDUCT

When I walk into an office and the secretary says, "What do you need?"
Correcting someone about their mistakes in front of the whole group - embarrassing!
Classmate using foul and unprofessional language

POSITIVE PROFESSIONAL CONDUCT

When I walked into an office and the secretary says, "Good afternoon - How can I help you?"
Person talks TO you, not DOWN to you!
Co-worker knocking on door before entering

TIP #23
Thinking Blots

THEORY: This exercise was provided by Candice Hamilton-Miller of CHM Therapy Service (www.chmtherapy.com). She uses this activity for working with groups (families, couples, co-workers, kids, etc.) when dealing with family conflict, diversity training, cultural sensitivity, and bullying. The activity is designed to teach people to understand that everyone has their own perspective in a situation and that even with two people looking at the same image they often have very different views and interpretations.

IMPLEMENTATION:

Materials: (per maximum of 4 participants)

- One large piece of paper (poster size: 24x36 is ideal)
- Pots of finger paints (colors or just black is fine)
- One note pad and pen for each participant
- Timer

Instructions:

Fold the paper in half and crease the center line.

Open the paper and get each participant to put globs of paint on the same half of the paper – not to create any kind of picture, but more dots and lines and squiggles.

Now refold the paper, and create a mirror image inkblot.

Now unfold the paper and place each participant on a separate side of the paper, label each side (A, B, C, D).

Each participant now has a chance to write down whatever images they see or might see in the inkblot from their side of the paper within a set time limit. When the timer goes off, everyone moves around the paper to the next side and the process repeats. Once each person has written down what they see from each side of the paper, the activity moves to the processing phase.

PROCESSING: In this step, participants compare what they saw on each side, i.e. from each "perspective." If people describe the same image, ask them to check and point out where they saw it. Often people may see the same thing (a bird) without looking at the same blot view.

The discussion base of this activity will vary depending on your participants. The following questions may help:

1. Why do you think we all see things so differently?
2. What kinds of factors/experiences can influence how we see things?
3. How do you think this activity is like real life?

4. Have you ever been in a situation where you and another person have been in the same place and yet had very different versions of the situation?

5. What did people in your group do when you did not see the same image?

6. Knowing that we see things differently, how does this activity help you to change how you react in life?

Younger children often need more guidance in this discussion but are also equally perceptive in it. This activity is the perfect blend of cognitive and creative processes, and is equally suited to all age groups.

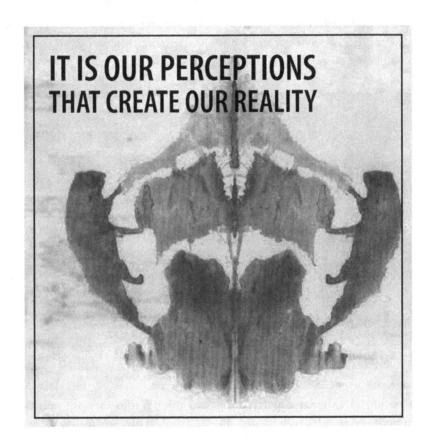

TIP #24

Treating Each Other at Least as Good as an Egg!

THEORY: Relationships are fragile. Handle with care...*like an EGG!* Years of trust and connectedness can be crushed with cruel words or actions. In our everyday life, it is not uncommon for people to lack sensitivity for how they treat others, especially when they're pre-occupied with their own issues and stress. This egg activity never fails to be very powerful with a group!

IMPLEMENTATION:
Materials:

- 1 raw egg
- 1 hard-boiled egg (clearly marked with a marker)
- Plastic tarp or table cloth (for dropping the raw egg)

Instructions: Without an explanation, pass out a raw egg and have people pass it around – you will notice they will pass it to one another *very* carefully.

After everyone has had a chance to pass the raw egg, then take out a hard-boiled egg and ask someone to catch it (only you know it is hard boiled!). They are usually taken by surprise, while catching the cooked egg.

You can reassure them that it is hard boiled, and thus can withstand more "toughness."

Then ask them to throw that (hard-boiled) one to one another. Ask them how they thought this activity related to relationships.

To really make a dramatic point, with the raw egg that was passed around, throw it onto a plastic tarp on the floor. Make the point that if we are rough with people's feelings and do not handle with care, feelings as well as relationships can be splattered and just like Humpty Dumpty, it will never go back the same way.

In the brainstorming, you might summarize with these points:

1. Relationships are fragile and we handle the egg more carefully than we do our relationships.
2. Treat one another like the raw egg. Even though we often treat one another like we are hard boiled–we ignore feelings and do not pay enough attention to handling each other gently.
3. Don't take others for granted. Spend more time nurturing your relationships. Take extra time and caution like you did when the egg was raw.
4. The hard-boiled egg was exposed to boiling water – that is how it became hard. We all can become hardened by adversity, but that does not mean you can toss each other around like there is no sensitivity. Handle with care!

PROCESSING: Are you more like the raw or hard-boiled egg? How do you treat those close to you? How do you treat others outside of your family and close friends? Did you handle the raw egg we passed around more gently than you handle your loved ones? How can you handle them with more care?

TIP #25

Role Play Variations…For People Who Hate Role Playing

THEORY: Most clients say they hate role playing, yet if I could think of the one main activity that I do to get clients to help them improve their interpersonal skills, it is role playing. I role play with my individual clients often, and break into role plays naturally when they are talking about relationship issues such as marital spats, family quarrels, trouble managing their children, or addressing a coworker.

IMPLEMENTATION: Rather than just talking about it, I give my clients practice showing me first how they either have or plan to communicate. I then use one of my assertive sheets, particularly the Guidelines for Being Assertive and the checklist to Stay Assertive (Chapter 7), to give some structure to evaluate their communication.

If I am working with a couple who had a difficult interaction, I have them role play the situation so we can dissect why it went wrong. Then, they role play the scene again (with some coaching), this time more assertively. I often ask my clients to switch sides, to help them understand the other's perspective. I play them, and they take on the role of the other person. I like to "mix it up" as to *who* is playing *who*.

With individual clients, sometimes I have them switch seats – even with me, so they can play the therapist. I particularly do this when I am having what I call a "dental session," telling them maybe they can do a better job than me in getting them to open up. It usually works, since they would prefer pushing themselves to talk more than switching seats and getting out of their comfort zone!

In a group situation, even in workplace trainings, I often have participants break up into small groups and role-play situations from their own lives, taking turns using their situations. This offers group support and practice trying out new behaviors in a setting where we all speak the same language! Sometimes I have other people in the group take the role of the person who is describing their situation, just as I do in my individual sessions. It helps everyone get different perspectives!

For a quick and easy group role play example, use notecards with the start of a sentence on them, such as, "Your child calls you a name and you say, -----." This offers great practice for speaking assertively without getting into personal situations. Another advantage to this is that group members can also comment on your non-verbals in order to give feedback as to how your verbals and your non-verbals match.

Another quick role play variation to show how to assert yourself without being aggressive is to have a simple role play scenario, such as someone being continually late, and have canned lines that the person reads while the therapist plays the one who was waiting. So even though they are role playing, it is very non-threatening, as they only are reading canned lines. After the canned responses are read, the group members are asked to give feedback on what was and was not assertive about the therapists' responses, using a communication handout from Chapter 7 as a guide.

When focusing on listening skills, a fun variation in a group or even with a client is to "play it up"–***not*** using active listening and going to this extreme makes it easier to distinguish hearing from active listening.

Tip: Whatever role play variation you use, a smartphone can be helpful to make a recording of a role play right then and there! If you split up into small groups for role play, have an observer in the group record the conversation using the person's phone whose situation it is so that he/she can observe later and get feedback on how they come across. If you have video connected to a computer, you can do the replay right in a small group.

PROCESSING: Role playing gives no shortage of opportunities to practice good communication. This provides feedback from others, role modeling if they are stuck, and the practice is invaluable to give clients ideas of how to respond in challenging situations. I often suggest to clients that they rehearse in front of a mirror to practice speaking assertively, especially if they need to speak in front of a group, and can then observe their verbal as well as their non-verbal communication. Practice, Practice, Practice!

TIP #26

Give Yourself a Hand!

THEORY: A great way to start off a group is to show the importance of flexible thinking, thereby setting the stage for starting the group off with an open mind. This is universally enjoyed in every group I have done, and makes an interesting impact on how we perceive things differently and what is comfortable for one person is not comfortable for another. The lesson of this exercise is that we need to keep an open mind because there are various ways people can be "right" – not only *our* way!

IMPLEMENTATION: Clasp your fingers so that your fingers interlock. Which thumb is on top? In a group situation, about half have their left thumb on top and half the right, regardless of right or left-handedness. Note what is natural for some is not natural for another. This represents our perceptions – we think people see things the same way and by this *hands on* exercise we realize this is not true! Now shift your fingers so they are intertwined the opposite way (make sure all fingers are clasped and intertwined differently, not just the thumbs). How does it feel? Common responses are "weird, strange, uncomfortable." However, for about half the group, it is effortless and natural! Thus, this exercise serves as a metaphor of how we need to shift our thinking so slightly in order to think in different ways. It can remind you also to be open-minded when you listen to others, rather than expecting them to see things your way. This helps people develop flexibility in being able to look at things in a different way, and realize that people do not often interpret things like us.

Want an advanced version? Try the same exercise with folding your arms the natural way, and then the opposite way. Again, a show of hands reveals that between 35-65 percent of people do not share your natural way of doing things.

Want another advanced version? Try the same exercise with crossing your legs! Which leg do you have on top? How does it feel when you switch so that the other one is one top? What might feel strange to you is very comfortable for some people!

PROCESSING: I use this powerful demonstration with my clients individually to emphasize the importance of flexible thinking and realizing that many people do not think or react naturally like them. A group setting is particularly powerful, since clients can actually see how many people do not have their same "defaults." Brainstorming with your group on what they learned from this exercise often brings up many different and interesting points. Underlying it all is helping people realize that our way is not the only way, and certainly not the only *right* way!

WHEN YOU THINK FLEXIBILITY, **YOU FOCUS ON POSSIBILITIES** AND NOT **LIMITATIONS.**

TIP #27

What Are Your Accomplishments?

THEORY: This is a very upbeat, simple exercise for groups to combine individual exploration with developing social cohesiveness by sharing with others. It gives people an opportunity to reflect on positive things about themselves and share them with others!

IMPLEMENTATION: I like combining self-reflection with social interaction. Start off with asking people to write down at least 5 things they have accomplished that make them proud. Then ask them to stand up and find someone in the group so that both can share their lists. After a couple minutes have them share their lists with a new partner. After a few pairings, have them sit back in their seats and then share with their table or the person sitting next to them, or the group as a whole, how it felt to focus on positive things about themselves and how it felt to share those things with others.

PROCESSING: Even though this exercise seems quite simple, it has the potential to make a profound impact on group participants who often are afraid of "tooting their horn" and it also gives people permission to be proud of themselves and express it to others! I have been amazed at how powerful this simple exercise is in developing assertiveness and confidence by being encouraged to reflect on strengths and accomplishments, since all too often people focus on the negative. Sharing our accomplishments with someone else can really make an impression! An adage to sum this exercise up at the end of the session to leave your participants with is *"How you can really love others until you really love yourself?"*

THE SECRET OF BEING ABLE
TO REALLY LOVE OTHERS
IS LOVING YOURSELF FIRST!
AFTER ALL, HOW CAN YOU GIVE ANYTHING TO OTHERS
THAT YOU DON'T ALREADY HAVE YOURSELF?

    Judith Belmont, MS (2013) • 127 More Amazing TIPS and TOOLS for the Therapeutic Toolbox: DBT, CBT and Beyond • www.belmontwellness.com

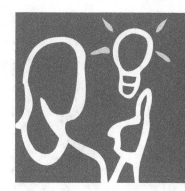

TIP #28

Get Active with Cognitive Behavior Therapy TIPs and Tools

THEORY: Cognitive Behavior Therapy, known as CBT, is an active psychotherapeutic approach that considers faulty thinking to be the root of many psychological problems. It is widely adopted and the fastest growing therapeutic orientation in the world today. The approach has been clinically tested in thousands of ways and its effectiveness for dealing with a wide range of psychological issues has been substantiated. Results for dealing with symptoms such as anxiety and depression have been shown to be dramatic, especially in short term therapy. CBT's practical skill-based focus is extremely powerful in treating commonly encountered psychological issues such as low self-esteem, depression and anxiety. The success is largely due to CBT's strong psycho-educational component, requiring an active role by the therapist to teach clients how to identify and change maladaptive thought patterns. This life skills orientation is best supplemented in between sessions with handouts, worksheets and CBT-inspired books to support clients in their attempts to change unhealthy thinking habits.

The underlying notion behind CBT is that although we cannot change the way we feel directly, we can change the way we think, which in turn changes the way we feel, which in turn changes the way we behave!

Albert Ellis developed Rational Emotive Therapy (RET) in the 1950s. It was Aaron Beck in the 1960s that developed Ellis' model further to coin the term Cognitive Therapy. By the 1970s, these two pioneers somewhat independently influenced a new wave of treatment which is one of the most popular in present day, known generally as Cognitive Behavior Therapy. Cognitive Therapy seemed to be a middle ground between the approaches of Behaviorism and Psychoanalytic therapy, since it combined "mentalistic" concepts with observable and measurable treatment, while focusing on making practical changes.

Despite the fact that CBT has emerged only in the last half century, the roots of cognitive behavior theory go back as far as the Roman Empire, when Epictetus, considered as one of history's famous examples of Stoicism, said,

"It's not what happens to you, but how you react to it that matters."

AND

"People are not disturbed by things, but by the view they take of them."

Many philosophers, poets, and great thinkers throughout all ages alluded to the cornerstone of CBT thought, i.e. that our adjustment to life is pretty much dependent on our thoughts and our attitudes.

IMPLEMENTATION: The following sixteen TIPs are handouts and worksheets that will help you teach your clients how to change their self-talk, and subsequently change their lives. CBT has a very heavy emphasis on homework, including psycho-educational handouts and worksheets to teach clients practical ways to reduce their cognitive distortions. In this CBT section, I have tried to crystallize the main points of CBT for your clients in handouts. Hopefully with the material in this section, you will have new teaching and processing tools for use with your clients to reinforce CBT principles with the underlying belief that if you change your thoughts, you can change your life!

PROCESSING: CBT has been a life-changer for countless clients who have been unable to control persistent thoughts of low self-esteem, negativity, depression and anxiety. These feelings have impacted their life adjustment as well as the quality of their relationships and personal and professional success. CBT has given the tools to help people change their well ingrained habits of thinking and behavior.

Although there is a place in therapy for insight and making peace with your past, sometimes, *knowing better* does not mean that we can actually *do better*. If so, we would all be exercising regularly and be in great shape! For many clients, no matter how much they know they are not *thinking right,* they remain stuck. Why? Without CBT resources, they did not know how to transform old patterns of thinking to new ones!

Therapists who focus on supporting and listening, to the exclusion of actively educating, will not be able to offer a foundation of skills to help the client make changes. Both are necessary for some clients to really *get better.*

I have been struck by comments from fellow therapists that they would rather have the client come upon insights on their own, and are afraid of being too directive. Some therapists regard any type of teaching as being too directive and synonymous with telling the client what to do. This is far from the truth. Teaching does not mean telling! Rather, it means teaching your client strategies that they have never learned in school or in life. This proactive approach empowers clients with tools for life. Experiential exercises and the use of metaphors help jar old ways of thinking and often break through even the most strongly-erected unhealthy habits and defenses.

As Confucius said so aptly, *"Teach me and I will forget, show me and I will remember, involve me and I will understand."*

Note: All of these self-help assignments are quick and easy, yet can be very self-empowering, especially with the guidance of a therapist who can support the new self-empowering language. They will help clients be more proactive and responsible for their own growth and wellness. Self-help assignments transform *what* into *how*. All of the following 17 TIPS are great as stand-alone TIPS or they can be used as a systematized menu to follow with your client or group so they can become familiar with a sampler of resources with a strong Cognitive Behavioral orientation.

TIP #29

Do You Know Your Psychological ABCs?

By the fact that you are reading this, it is clear you have mastered your basic ABCs in school! Now to learn the psychological ABCs!

This handout will help you learn your psychological ABCs, based on the work of Albert Ellis, the founder of Rational Emotive Therapy (RET). RET has helped people from around the world learn how to change negative thoughts and replace them with more positive ones. The underlying concept of RET is that most psychological problems are caused by faulty ways of thinking, and his model demonstrates how to break a situation down to distinguish between thoughts, feelings and situations which often are bundled in one big confusion in times of stress.

The psychological ABCs will help you separate your thoughts from feelings so you can replace negative thoughts with more healthy ways of thinking, which will result in healthier feelings and behaviors.

First, let's take a common situation – fear of speaking up in groups. Take the case of my client, Jean, who got anxious before her weekly workplace team meetings due to her fear of speaking up in groups. After the meeting, she would be very frustrated with herself for not speaking her mind, which led to self-loathing and anxiety. It had become a vicious cycle and she came to counseling to gain more confidence with asserting herself at work as well as at home. She was tired of living in fear of what other people thought.

Teaching her the psychological ABCs helped her learn the tools to tackle her anxiety and harness the thoughts that caused anxiety. Here is what she learned using the RET model:

A – Activating event: Weekly staff meeting discussions in which I might be called upon unexpectedly or might have an idea I want to contribute.

B – Beliefs: "I might be unprepared when they call on me – and I don't want to look stupid. I would NEVER be able to face my coworkers again if I blow it! That would be TERRIBLE! I HATE being unprepared!"

C – Consequences: Feelings and behavior

Feelings – Anxiety, nervousness

Behavior and behavioral reactions – Keeping quiet, tightness in throat, being withdrawn

So…did the weekly staff meetings cause her to be anxious? NO! It was her beliefs that were extreme and irrational. Look at all of her all-or-nothing choice of words such as HATE, TERRIBLE, NEVER and her negative assumptions that she might seem stupid. She is thinking negatively and is thinking the worst. What if she disputed this negative way of thinking? That is where "D" comes in!

D – Dispute the beliefs: The challenging thoughts for disputing are: Why would I think I might sound stupid? Have I thought I might actually sound smart? Anyway, even if I say something that is wrong, that does not mean that people will think I am stupid, and it does not mean I am stupid. That is generalizing and blowing things out of proportion. I am not a fortune teller!

E – Effect: For Jean, by disputing her irrational thoughts, the effect of the more rational way of thinking was that she could calm down and stop being anxious about speaking up in groups. The more she worked on disputing her irrational self-talk, the more she was able to speak up, to the point where she looked forward to the meetings so that she could actively work on developing her confidence in speaking up, which helped her improve her self-confidence overall. By practicing her psychological ABCs, she felt happier and more confident in her life in general!

TIP #30
Using Your Psychological ABCs!

Now it's your turn! Think of a situation that poses some difficulty for you, one that triggers some anxiety, excessive anger or feelings of depression. Dissect your thoughts, feelings and behaviors as in the previous example, and dispute it!

Change your thoughts and you will change your life!

A - Activating Event

_____

B - Beliefs (Irrational Beliefs and Thoughts)

_____

_____

C - Consequence (Comprised of Feelings and Behaviors)

Feelings _____

Behaviors _____

D - Dispute (Dispute the Irrational Thoughts)

_____

_____

E - Effect of More Rational Thinking

_____

_____

Congratulations! Don't you feel better already?

Judith Belmont, MS (2013) • 127 More Amazing TIPS and TOOLS for the Therapeutic Toolbox: DBT, CBT and Beyond • www.belmontwellness.com • All rights reserved

TIP #31

My Psychological ABCs Diary

We all recognize that knowing what is good for us is one thing, but being able to act on it is another thing. It takes practice, and lots of it! That is why it is important to keep practicing your psychological ABCs. Keeping a log to help you practice will help you replace your irrational beliefs with more rational ones.

Watch out for the stories you tell yourself! *Sometimes they are really big whoppers!*

Use this as a daily log to get you in the right frame of mind to master your thoughts, and thereby master your moods! Keeping this diary/log will provide you the structure to differentiate situations, thoughts and feelings to live a life where you can *Think Straight to Feel Great!*

My Psychological ABCs Diary

Activating Event	Beliefs	Consequence (Feelings & Behavior)	Disputing	Effect of Disputing
Boyfriend broke up with me	I'm nothing without him - I can't stand it!	Devastated, overeats, isolates self, can't concentrate	I don't need anyone to make me feel worthy. There will be others.	Seek support, connect, share feelings, sad but not immobilized, can focus on living

TIP #32

Is It an A, B or C? Don't Jumble Your Letters!

Sometimes it is not so easy to differentiate the psychological ABCs.

For the following items, put the letter that corresponds with each item. Then check your answers with the key below.[1]

A next to an activating event or situation

B next to beliefs

C next to consequence (comprised of feelings and behavior)

_____ I feel like you are so inconsiderate!

_____ I am embarrassed!

_____ I become withdrawn.

_____ My spouse cheated on me.

_____ I am in a meeting where I need to lead a presentation.

_____ I am too nervous to speak up.

_____ What if I make a fool of myself?

_____ Things will never be much different - it's hopeless!

_____ I am afraid to say something stupid - it would be so embarrassing!

_____ She should not have said that!

_____ I hear an old song that I associate with my old boyfriend.

_____ I feel sad when I hear that song now.

_____ He makes me feel so angry!

_____ I will make a plan to exercise and get into shape.

_____ I will never love anyone like that again![1]

---

[1]ANSWER KEY: 1. B 2.C 3.C 4.A 5.A 6.C 7.B 8.B 9.B 10.B 11.A 12.C 13.B 14.C 15.B

NOTE: Some answers might be surprising. For example, in the case of number 1, just because the phrase is "I feel" you are inconsiderate it does not mean it is a feeling - actually it is a thought!

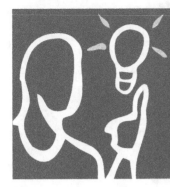

Stating an Interpretation as Fact

"I can't say this to her because she doesn't like to talk about it."

Personalizing

"If he ignores me, then I must have done something wrong!"

Making Comparisons

"She is so much smarter than me."

"Compared to him, I am a loser."

Confusing Fact with Interpretation

"I know for a fact that he does not care about me."

Blowing Things Out of Proportion

"I can't believe how rude he always is to me – I will never get over it!"

"It will be awful if he does not call me back."

Being a Negative Mind Reader

"I know he said that because he feels sorry for me - he really thinks I'm a loser."

"He will never understand me – why do I bother to try?"

Being a Black and White Thinker

"He's a bad person."

"He hates me."

Rigid, Perfectionistic Thinking

"He should not act that way."

"I should be much further along in my life by now."

"She ought to have done this instead."

Being a "Know-It-All"

"I know this will be a disaster."

"I knew he would act like that!"

"Nothing will ever change!"

Labeling

"She is just lazy."

"I am so stupid."

Overgeneralizing

"All men are like that."

"You can't trust anyone – people just use you."

"Everyone only cares about themselves."

Powerless Victimization

"He makes me feel that way."

"She makes me so mad!"

"I can't change my life."

"He ruined me."

"I can't help it."

Self-Blaming

"It's all my fault that my child has so many problems."

"I ruined our relationship."

Being a Negative "Yeah, But-Head!"

"Yeah, I guess it was okay, but I really hate it."

"Yeah, but he doesn't know what he is talking about."

Seeing Things as Permanent Rather Than Temporary

"I am always depressed and things never work out. The story of my life!"

Being a Fortune Teller

"I will always be alone!"

"He will get tired of me!"

TIP #34
Categorizing Your Negative Thoughts

Using the handout in TIP 33 as a guide, write an example from your own life that demonstrates each type of thinking that applies to you.

Stating an Interpretation as Fact

_____

Personalizing

_____

Making Comparisons

_____

Confusing Fact with Interpretation

_____

Blowing Things Out of Proportion

_____

Being a Negative Mind Reader

_____

Being a Black and White Thinker

_____

Rigid, Perfectionistic Thinking

_____

Being a "Know-It-All"

_____

Labeling

Overgeneralizing

Powerless Victimization

Self-Blaming

Being a Negative "Yeah, But-Head!"

Seeing Things as Permanent Rather Than Temporary

Being a Fortune Teller

TIP #35

10 Minutes a Day to Change Your Thoughts From Automatic to Manual

For those who have driven a car with automatic transmission for years, and then try to learn how to drive a car with manual transmission, it can be quite challenging! The same thing occurs when trying to change our automatic thoughts!

The car analogy helps us understand how changing our automatic thoughts is far from easy. So often in life, our automatic thoughts serve as a "default," and if these automatic thoughts happen to be irrational, they end up being counterproductive. We often have no clue they are irrational!

This worksheet will help you go from automatic to manual! At the end of each day, why not take ten minutes and write down at least ten 'automatic' thoughts that went through your mind that were negative and/or irrational. That should not be difficult because most people have hundreds of negative thoughts a day. Negative thoughts do not merely mean that you don't like something. Rather, negative thoughts are distorted, irrational thoughts that are often so automatic we think they are true and factual. By reviewing at the end of each day your automatic negative thoughts and replace them with more positive thoughts, with daily practice, driving your thoughts on manual will become automatic!

Shift from Automatic to Manual! Replace your Negative Thinking with Positive Thinking!

	Automatic Negative Thinking	Positive Thinking
Example	I don't know how to talk to people.	Up until now, it has been hard for me to express myself confidently, and I am working on that now.
1		
2		
3		
4		
5		
6		
7		
8		
9		
10		

TIP #36

The 8 Thought Habits to Stop NOW!

"Stop acting as if life is a rehearsal. Live this day as if it were your last. The past is over and gone. The future is not guaranteed."

— *Wayne Dyer*

Are you undermining your life happiness with bad habits that you just can't seem to shake? Although we *know better*, old habits are hard to break. However, if we can't shake these negative thought habits, we live life as if we have smudgy glasses.

So clean those glasses, and **STOP** these eight common thought habits that lead us astray!

1. STOP expecting the world to fall into place the way you think it "should." Even though we all know life is not fair, we still find ourselves often expecting it to be! The more "shoulds" and expectations you have, the more you will be stuck in preconditions to happiness.

2. STOP taking yourself too seriously. As Carol Burnett said, *"Life is too serious to be taken seriously."* The more you see the humor and lightness in life, the lighter you will feel and the more you will be able to "lighten up" with others.

3. STOP thinking you know what is best for you. We often do not really know what is best for us – sometimes what does not turn out turns out to be just what we need!

4. STOP living life like you are going to live forever. Of course we all know we are going to die, but it remains often a theoretical construct. We end up taking things for granted and get enraged at what could be slight annoyances like too much rain on your beach vacation.

5. STOP asking so many *whys*. *"Why do these things happen to me?"* One of my favorite mottos is, 'It's just not wise to ask too many whys.' *"Why"* keeps you stuck in the past. Shift your focus from *"why"* to *"what's next?"*

6. STOP over-thinking things. Just like a car stuck in the mud, the more you spin your tires the deeper in the mud they go. The same type of thinking and perseveration that got you into a problem will not likely get you out of the problem.

7. STOP trying to change others. Stop trying to change someone's mind or teach anyone anything unless that person is a willing student. You'll never be able to teach if someone does not want to learn – especially if it's about how right you are!

8. STOP blaming others for things that are not going right with your life. Stop renting others so much space in your head! ***Time to evict!*** Get better, not bitter.

So once you STOP these toxic thought habits, how about using this as a FRESH START to live the rest of your life with much more wisdom, positivity, and happiness? Don't you deserve it?

TIP #37

Thoughts That I Need to Stop NOW!

Look at the unhealthy 8 Thought Habits in TIP #36, and pick one thought habit to use as an example for this worksheet.

What about this habit makes it difficult to STOP?

_____

Think of at least two strategies to STOP that habit.

_____

What can you learn about yourself from the item that you picked?

_____

How would life be different if you could fully STOP that habit?

_____

What is the thought habit to replace the negative thought?

_____

What can you do to START NOW with the more positive thought habit?

_____

The last paragraph of TIP 36 suggests using this as a FRESH START to live the rest of your life with much more wisdom, positivity and happiness. The question posed was, "Don't you deserve it?" What was your answer? (If low self-esteem has made you think you don't deserve it – write why.)

_____

What new thoughts can you use to replace the old thought habits?

_____

Name three things you can do every day, STARTING NOW!

1. _____

2. _____

3. _____

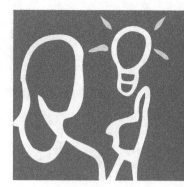

TIP #38
Don't Be a Negative Story Teller!

Do you tell yourself lies and stories, and not even know you are doing it?

Watch what you're thinking! People get depressed, they get negative, and they get anxious for generally one main reason—they treat interpretations like facts!

Consider the following examples and then in the right column, change the distorted interpretations to facts.

Interpretations	Facts
Things always go wrong.	*I am often disappointed in the way things are going, and I will try to look for the positive side.*
He makes me so mad.	
I can't change how I feel.	
I'll never love again.	
It's all my fault.	
I'm a loser.	
I should be further along in my life.	

Notice the distorted thinking, and irrational words such as "always, never, can't, should" and the fortune telling in the phrase, "I'll never love again." How can anyone predict the future with certainty? That is fiction, not fact!

In the following examples, notice how the fact shows a much more positive way of thinking. What makes the difference? ATTITUDE! There is nothing wrong with interpretations, but at least know they are not facts! Think of a fiction book: We know it is not supposed to be true! We know it is just a story.

However, in life, we tell ourselves so many stories, that after a while, we lose sight of the fact that they are stories. We think they are true even though sometimes they are actually big whoppers! We wouldn't lie to anyone else like that!

Reminder: There is nothing wrong with storytelling – *just know you are telling stories!* If you are telling yourself *fiction*, don't talk yourself into thinking that it is *non-fiction!*

So for most people in life, what are the facts we can believe in? Here is just a sampling:

    Fact #1: *The more you feel depressed and hopeless, the more stories you tell yourself.*

    Fact #2: *The more extreme anxiety you have in the absence of real danger, the more stories you tell yourself.*

    Fact #3: *The more time you spend in bitterness and blame (including self-blame), the more stories you tell yourself.*

    Fact #4: *The more you don't like yourself, the more stories you tell yourself.*

    Fact #5: *The more you live in the land of "woulda, coulda, shoulda," the more stories you tell yourself.*

Client Example of Confusing Fact with Fiction

'Jenny' told me she blames the difficulty that she has with her children on her own unruly behavior in her teens, especially her sexual promiscuity. She felt she was being punished for her past, and was being "paid back." Jenny feels like she is doomed and that life will never be better for her. She feels like she ruined her family's life and that she should have never had children. Jenny claims she can't stand herself, and thinks that nobody else likes her either, not even her husband! She reasons that she can't change the past, so her life will never change.

Jenny felt this way despite the fact that at the ripe age of 45 she had been leading a responsible, law-abiding life as a mother, wife, and school teacher for 20 years! Her lack of self-forgiveness for her past behavior loomed larger than life, even though those behaviors were in the distant past.

Based on the client example, consider the following questions.

1. What are some examples of Jenny confusing fact with fiction?

2. What are some of the words she used that indicate that this is fiction and not fact? Underline each one.

3. Do you notice the words like "can't," "should," and "never?" Do you notice the labels? What are they?

4. Are there stories that you also tell yourself that are not true? What are they?

TIP #39
More Fact Or Fiction Takeaways

Separate Fact from Fiction Takeaways

- Many thoughts we treat as facts are really interpretations.
- Many interpretations are so automatic we do not know they are not fact.
- Examine your thought habits so that you are aware of your "default" way of thinking–only then can you change.
- As you stop believing your own negative fantasyland, you will feel more positive and empowered.
- Realize when you are just telling yourself stories! Nothing is wrong with being a storyteller–just know when you are!
- Stop upsetting yourself with nonsense that you believe to be true.
- Stop over-catastrophizing and making mountains out of molehills.
- Refuse to feel like a victim and feel more like a victor.
- Be more solution-focused and not problem-focused.

Activity to Separate Fact from Fiction

Keep a magnifying glass to remind you to be a "thought detective" to look beyond what you are thinking and identify distorted thinking that is fiction rather than fact. Remind yourself that when we interpret, we are telling ourselves stories. There is nothing wrong with stories–but just know that they are not real or true!

So take your magnifying glass and identity your thought habits–and make sure you can distinguish between the stories you tell yourself and the actual facts at hand!

Now it's your turn: What stories do you tell yourself? Below write three of your self-sabotaging whoppers and then replace them with more gentle and kind facts.

Fiction	Fact
1	1
2	2
3	3

 Judith Belmont, MS (2013) • 127 More Amazing TIPS and TOOLS for the Therapeutic Toolbox: DBT, CBT and Beyond • www.belmontwellness.com •

TIP #40

20 Tips to Be Miserable

1. Hold grudges - Focus on "who's right" and how someone should be more like you!

2. Blow things out of proportion and make mountains out of molehills. Life is so much more dramatic that way!

3. Think that you are a "know-it-all," including being able to predict the future, knowing when things are utterly hopeless, and not budging from your convictions!

4. Depend on someone for your happiness. Then you have a right to expect all sorts of things from them – after all, your happiness depends on it!

5. Keep reworking the past – maybe, just maybe, it will start getting better!

6. Try to change things that are out of your control. With the belief that if you persist long enough, you can change anything you want, you won't stop trying. After all, quitting is for losers!

7. Be more of a judger than a lover. After all, if you judge others and they fall short of your expectations, what is there really to love? Don't they want to get better – like you?

8. Refuse to be happy until everything falls into place in your life. If you stop in the land of "good enough" that would be accepting mediocrity.

9. Be nice above all, even if you have to give up your own dreams so you can support the dreams of others. Otherwise you would be selfish!

10. Make sure everyone likes you – after all, who wants to hang around with a loser? (Of course, miserable people love to label!)

11. Forget about self-care and eating in moderation – life's too short to deny yourself!

12. Calm yourself with non-prescription drugs or alcohol – feel the buzz!

13. Harbor resentment for anyone in your life who has wronged you – they don't deserve your forgiveness! That'll teach them!

14. Be ungrateful – after all, with all the poverty and conflict in the world, what in the world is there to be grateful for?

15. Don't change! Stay with what is comfortable – otherwise you might not know what you are getting into!

16. Don't read any more self-help handouts – *what do they know anyway?*

17. Don't ask for help or support – you don't want to get hurt and you certainly don't want to seem weak!

18. Help people who aren't asking for help. For example, if someone needs to get feedback on why they are acting like a jerk, aren't you doing them a favor by *setting them straight?*

19. Be brutally honest! If someone can't take the truth that's their fault – you're just telling it like it is! Wouldn't the world be a better place if people stopped beating around the bush and sugar-coating everything?

20. Stop making lists like this one – all this self-help nonsense is for losers!

Can you think of other ways to be miserable to add to this list?

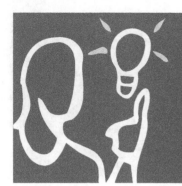

TIP #41

Stop Getting in Your Own Way – Thoughts to Change NOW!

Is your thinking out of control? Notice the words in bold below showing exaggerated, "out of control" thinking. Nothing but the most life altering, debilitating situations merit those types of extreme thoughts. When we talk ourselves down from these exaggerated, immobilizing thoughts, we can handle life much better! When you "terribilize" and "awfulize" things that are really just annoying, unfortunate and troubling, you give too much power to others and your own negative way of thinking and you will keep getting in your own way!

Here is a list to help you change unhealthy thoughts to healthy ones.

Unhealthy Thoughts	Healthy Thoughts
I **can't** help myself!	I can learn ways to help myself, though it's hard.
It's **terrible** that he said that!	I was very angry when he said that!
He **shouldn't** be that way!	I wish he was not that way.
She **never** listens to me!	She seems disinterested when I speak.
I am such a **loser.**	I've had many setbacks, and will learn from them.
He drives people **crazy**!	Many people find him difficult to talk to.
I will be happy **if only**…	I will try to be happy no matter what!
It's her **fault** I am the way I am.	She has triggered some of my negativity, but I am in charge of how I react.
I will **never** forgive her.	It will be hard to forgive her.
He **has to** see the harm he has caused.	I would like him to understand how hurtful his actions were to me.

So stop getting in your own way by:

- Treating interpretations like facts
- Judging yourself and others
- Blowing things out of proportion
- Expecting that life should be fair!
- Negatively labeling yourself and others
- Holding grudges

Can you think of other things that you do that get in your own way? For every answer that you write, how about thinking of a solution so that you can stop getting in your own way?

 Judith Belmont, MS (2013) • 127 More Amazing TIPS and TOOLS for the Therapeutic Toolbox: DBT, CBT and Beyond • www.belmontwellness.com •

TIP #42

Rational Thinking at Work!

Separating rational from irrational thinking will also help you in your work life! Consider these common rational and irrational beliefs, and then fill in your own examples.

Irrational Beliefs	Rational Beliefs
It's awful to make mistakes.	It's normal to make mistakes, and I'll learn from them.
My co-worker is so much more well-liked than me.	I am not in a race – I can learn from her to improve myself.
I hate when they show me up!	Their success does not diminish me.
They have to like me!	My self-worth does not depend on whether they like me.
I couldn't stand to be fired!	It would be unfortunate, but it does not define my life.
I HATE this job!	I am unhappy in this job.
My boss is an idiot!	I do not respect my boss very much.
I feel like a failure.	I am not happy with my progress.
This is a crappy job.	I don't like this job and am going to look for another one.

Activity: Fill in your own irrational beliefs that get in the way at work, and then respond with a more rational alternative.

Irrational Belief	Rational Alternative

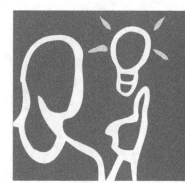

TIP #43

Schedule a Worry Time

Worry appears to be a favorite pastime of some people. No matter how much they try, they cannot seem to stop worrying. Much of the worry has to do with events in their future, due to uncertainty and fear that things are not going to turn out well. However, just as focusing too much on the past robs you of the present, a tendency to worry about the future or things out of your control limits your pleasure of life now. The thing about worry is that if you look back and think about what you worried about two years ago, do you remember the specifics? Do you keep replacing one worry with another? Time to kick the habit!

This is what worry does to your mental health:

> It keeps you stuck in the land of *"what ifs?"*
>
> It robs you of today.
>
> It robs you of feeling empowered.
>
> It makes you lose your confidence and leads to self-doubt
>
> You end up taking yourself – and life itself – way too seriously, since it is hard to "lighten up" when you are a worrywart.

ACTIVITY: Use an hourglass timer and give yourself a "time out" for 2 or 3 minutes. Let yourself think of all the worries that you have, and give yourself that time to obsess. Okay – maybe you can turn the hourglass over once more if you are not finished! Once the sands are all gone, that is your trigger to compartmentalize your worry and go about your day with an attitude of gratitude. A timer in your kitchen or at your desk at work will remind you of the need to limit your negative thinking and give it a time limit! Otherwise the worry can keep going on and on and on....

WORRY IS LIKE A ROCKING CHAIR.

NO MATTER HOW FAST YOU GO,

AND HOW MUCH YOU ROCK,

YOU NEVER REALLY GET ANYWHERE.

TIP #44

Keep a Worry Outcome Diary

Therapist and mental health writer, Bobbi Emel, who has a terrific site, *The Bounce Blog* (thebounceblog.com), finds this **Worry Outcome Diary** helpful with her clients, based on the work of Borkovec, Hazlett-Stevens, & Diaz (1999).[2]

How Realistic Is Your Worry?

This tool assists you in keeping track of what you worry about so that you can see if your worries are realistic or not.

Specifically, it looks like this:

1. My worry:
2. What outcome (end result) do I fear:
3. How bad would this outcome be on a scale of 0-10 (0 = not bad at all, 10 = the worst thing that could happen):
4. What really happened:
5. How bad was the real outcome (same 0-10 scale as above):

Find a notebook and jot down these entries or copy and paste the above several times onto separate pages on your computer.

Then, throughout the day:

1. Note each thing that you are worried about.
2. Write down what you think will happen that is so bad or scary about each worry.
3. Rate on a scale from 0-10 how bad this feared outcome would be.

At the end of each day, review your diary to see if your worries were realistic:

4. Write down what really happened to the thing you worried about.
5. Finally, rate the real outcome on the same scale of 0-10.

Now compare numbers 3 and 5. Was the outcome as bad as you feared? Most likely not.

Even if you do this Worry Outcome Diary for a week or two, you will soon find out that you can stop worrying about most of the things on your worry list because they're not true! Or at least the outcome–the very thing that you spent so much time and energy worrying about–wasn't anywhere near as bad as you thought it would be!

---

[2]The role of positive beliefs about worry in generalized anxiety disorder and its treatment. *Clinical Psychology and Psychotherapy, 6,* 126-138.

Dialectical Behavior Therapy (DBT) Made Easy

TIPS 45–68

4

TIP #45

Introduction to DBT

THEORY: Dialectical Behavior Therapy is a life-skills therapeutic approach combining Eastern and Western psychological frameworks. In this comprehensive model of treating even the most treatment resistant clients, the Eastern focus of *Mindfulness* and *Acceptance* is combined with the Western change-based approach of Cognitive Behavioral Psychology. Thus, you might say B.F. Skinner and Buddha cross paths in this *East meets West* model of treatment. A Cognitive Behavioral focus is softened with the seemingly opposed concepts of Mindfulness and Acceptance.

DBT is a skills-based approach, offering practical life skills tools for both individual and group therapy. Skills practice through various techniques which are outlined in this chapter provides the cornerstone of DBT's success. DBT focuses on skill building in 4 basic areas: The two *change-based* areas are *Emotional Regulation* and *Interpersonal Skill Building*, and the two *acceptance-based* areas are *Mindfulness* and *Distress Tolerance*.

DBT is a relatively new model, developed by Dr. Marsha Linehan in the early 1990s. Although relatively new in the field, many of the facets of DBT have been widely adopted in various mental health settings where practical life skill building is a priority. As a psychologist at the University of Washington, she initially studied and worked with highly suicidal clients. Due to this population's difficulty in coping with life's stresses and generally poor impulse control under stress, she developed very simple skills for them to regularly practice to gain more self-control over impulsive behavior. These suicidal clients were generally diagnosed as having Borderline Personality Disorder, which then became the focus of Lineman's study and treatment.

Recognizing the difficulty of Borderlines to cope with their intense and conflicting emotions, combined with poor impulse control and possible suicidal intent, she developed a series of life skills coping strategies through education, worksheets and handouts. Her well-known teaching guide for clinicians leading DBT groups, *Skills Training Manual for Treating Borderline Personality Disorder*, is her blueprint for leading highly structured DBT psychosocial skill building groups. Her web site, BehavioralTech.org offers many resources.

Linehan does have her own certification program to use the DBT model, but use of her material is now so widespread due to the applicability of her resources to any clinician looking to provide clients with "hands on" life skills strategies, that many clinicians can apply the "user-friendly" DBT techniques quite effectively without formal training. For example, with her step-by-step manual providing a very specific structure to her psychosocial skills training groups, non-traditionally DBT trained clinicians have included DBT work in their own practices. Her DBT groups are very structured and systematic. Each of the 8 session groups have a certain life skills topic and materials to focus on for each unit. So, for example, her classic group format outlined in her skills manual for session #4 in Oregon would be theoretically the same as in Boston. This allows for consistency within the DBT model. The structure also allows for clients to retake or watch videos of certain sessions over and over again to reinforce skills in certain areas of need.

Due to the universality of issues that so many of our clients present, Linehan's work has offered a prolific amount of tools in any clinician's toolbox to help improve life coping skills. Thus, in this chapter I will refer to Linehan's classic work as well as offshoots of the classic DBT model. Some new variations have been alluded to as *the new wave of DBT* (Lane Pederson, Psy.D., LP, DBTC) or *innovative DBT* (Cathy Moonshine, Ph.D., MAC, CADC III). DBT strategies have been made popular by various clinicians in the field, who were either trained or inspired by the DBT model, including Thomas Marra, Ph.D., Cathy Moonshine, Ph.D., Lane Pederson, Psy.D., and Scott Spradlin, MA. All of these psychologists offer excellent DBT life skills training books, and this chapter on DBT will highlight some of the landmark DBT TIPS, along with some variations of Psychosocial Training ideas within the general DBT model.

Interestingly enough, Linehan's passion for DBT arose out of her own personal experience with Borderline Personality Disorder. In a 2011 speech at Hartford, Connecticut's Institute of Living, she disclosed that she was a patient there herself for over 2 years in her late teens. Habitually suicidal and diagnosed with social withdrawal and schizophrenia, she was kept in a seclusion room at times there because of her obsessive desire to self-mutilate and die.

Thus, the strategies that have developed came out of her own personal struggle and perhaps that is why they have served as such a comfort to countless individuals worldwide and have also helped save countless lives from suicide. As she reported, *"My whole experience of these episodes was that someone else was doing it; it was like 'I know this is coming, I'm out of control, somebody help me; where are you, God?' I felt totally empty, like the Tin Man; I had no way to communicate what was going on, no way to understand it."* After her discharge she ended up having some profound spiritual revelations and ended up completing a Ph.D. in Psychology from Loyola University.

IMPLEMENTATION: DBT is a behavioral approach which addresses the "dialectics" in everyday life. Dialectics stand for things that appear to be in conflict, or seem opposite. For instance, a client might have impulsive behaviors but still come to treatment to get better. In everyday life, loved ones argue and have conflict, when all they really want to do is get along and get closer.

Such are the paradoxes of life! People are constantly caught in the dialectics of everyday living, with conflicting thoughts and emotions. DBT strategies, both with the classic Linehan model and with newer approaches as part of the *new wave of DBT* strategies, are designed to help clients make peace with the paradoxes and their own conflicting needs and wants.

Common in the DBT approach is use of metaphors, visualizations and acronyms.

The four content areas within the DBT Model are as follows within two general areas: *Change* and *Acceptance*.

ACCEPTANCE-BASED SKILLS

- **Distress Tolerance** - Accepting things that are out of your control, tolerate stress
- **Core Mindfulness** - Being aware of being in the moment, being nonjudgmental of self and others

CHANGE-BASED SKILLS

Emotional Regulation - Solving problems and handling frustrations without impulsive behavior

Interpersonal Effectiveness Skills - learning skills for healthy relationships - communication, listening, etc.

PROCESSING: I am including some representative DBT TIPS in the four modules, which is just an introduction to the wealth of material available in the DBT area. For each of the modules, I will include a couple classic DBT tips from Linehan, and then include newer variations of the model by what Lane Pederson, Psy.D. terms as *the second wave of DBT*, and what Cathy Moonshine, Ph.D. terms as *innovative DBT.*

The beauty of the model is the broad spectrum that DBT encompasses, so many life skills tips and tools for groups and individuals from various disciplines can still fit into the DBT framework. The important idea to keep in mind is that DBT focuses on life skills education, providing structure to an active approach. It is geared to teach skills that can last a lifetime. Some of the following handouts are informational to explain DBT to your client, as well as for your own learning, while some of the other worksheets will give your client practice for skill building.

TIP #46

Dialectics Are Everywhere!

Dialectical Behavior Therapy is a treatment model that offers hope to countless individuals who are in need of practical life skills to live a healthy and productive life.

The foundation of the DBT model addresses the "dialectics" in everyday life. The term "dialectics" means things in life that are in conflict, or seemingly opposite, and need to be reconciled to fit together in some way to coexist peacefully. Even the premise of DBT embraces the two seemingly opposing ideas – the need to change with the need to be self-accepting.

Even though the ideas of change and acceptance seem to contradict one another, in the DBT model these apparent paradoxes are just what the model is all about – to bring opposite thoughts, feelings and emotions together to peacefully co-exist with one another.

Here are some common paradoxes in life that we all likely have seen either in ourselves or others:

- Pushing someone away when you really want to be close, for fear of being hurt.
- Feeling vulnerable and hurt, then acting aggressively and rudely. (In fact, hurt is often the root of anger – another dialectic!)
- Balancing your wants with your needs.
- Acting wrongly in order to prove that you are right!
- Being in conflict with people you love the most!
- Keeping your guard up to not get hurt, but that prevents you from letting people in!
- Sometimes you need to lose yourself to find yourself!
- We often need to loosen our grip to hold on to important relationships.
- Every door that closes brings another that opens.
- You get people out of your life, but still keep them in your head.
- The more you run away from something, the more it consumes – as the saying goes, "what you resist, will persist!"
- You say you accept your loved ones while trying to change them
- You depend on others while trying to prove your independence.
- Over-eating while dieting.
- Loving someone and treating them badly.
- Loving your spouse and having an affair.
- Loving your children but getting into conflicts and being critical of them.
- Feeling depressed so you drink alcohol excessively–also a depressant!
- You want to feel better so you self-medicate with drugs and alcohol.

- Loving others but hating yourself.
- Wanting to be healthy but eating poorly and neglecting self-care.
- Feeling calm on the outside and turbulent on the inside.

Dialectics are seen in books, too! Here are some mental health books as examples:

- *I Hate You, Don't Leave Me,* Hal Straus and Jerold J. Kreisman (1991)
- *Get Out of My Life, but First Could You Drive Me & Cheryl to the Mall,* Anthony Wolf, (1992)
- *The Enabler: When Helping Hurts the Ones You Love,* Angelyn Miller (2001)
- *Needy Greedy Love,* H.M. Mann (2011)
- *Codependent No More: How to Stop Controlling Others and Start Caring for Yourself,* Melody Beattie (1986)

Can you think of any dialectics of everyday life?

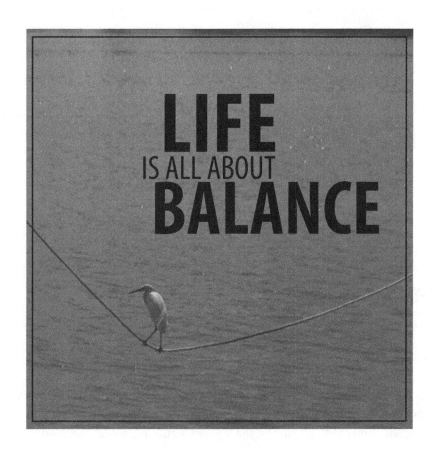

TIP #47
My Life's Dialectics!

In the previous TIP, dialectics are explained and many examples are given. Looking at the list above, are there some items that reflect your own life? If so, which ones can you relate to? One core dialectic we all need to confront is to balance ourselves physically and mentally in order to have a sense of well-being. How do you keep your balance?

What are some others dialectics in your life?

_____

_____

Of your own dialectics which you listed, which are adaptive and which ones are not adaptive?

_____

_____

How would you like to alter the maladaptive ones? What plan can you put into place?

_____

_____

Can you think of songs, advertisements, movies or TV shows that show dialectics?

_____

_____

NOTE: Life is a series of compromises between our opposing and sometimes conflicting wants and needs. Just like a seesaw or when we strive for a balance, we need to give up some things to get others. The more we are in tune with the delicate balance of our needs, wants and obligations, the higher functioning we can be. Nothing is black and white – we need to balance the shades of gray.

TIP #48

Acronyms Galore!

DBT is known for its use of acronyms. Acronyms are words that use each letter as initials to stand for a part of a sentence or a thought. Acronyms help people remember important concepts and have proved very useful in helping therapists and clients alike address important coping techniques. Acronyms give the therapist and client a common language to communicate complex concepts of various life skills strategies.

For many of the DBT TIPS, you will learn an acronym. To understand the DBT model is to familiarize yourself with its acronyms in one of the four content areas: *Emotional Regulation*, *Interpersonal Effectiveness*, *Distress Tolerance* and *Mindfulness*.

Using an acronym makes learning efficient. Many of the acronyms are used in a daily log for clients to put structure into their lives and keep them stabilized.

Example of a DBT acronym: One of Lineman's classic acronyms is MEDDSS. MEDDSS helps your client remember to be responsible to take not only medications regularly, but focus on other self-care areas.

The term MEDDSS stands for the skill and practice of self-help care:

> **M**astery
>
> **E**xercise
>
> **D**iet
>
> **D**rugs (prescription)
>
> **S**leep
>
> **S**pirituality

Thus, MEDDSS is an example of an acronym in a DBT Daily Diary (see TIP 68). The word diary is a bit misleading, as it typically has the connotation of writing something like a journal entry. The DBT diaries are basically a list of skills (represented by mostly acronyms) where check marks or circles are the only notations in the Diary. There is no narrative writing required, as the intention is to denote when the skills represented by various acronyms were practiced. It helps the individual stay focused on practicing and addressing various skills in attempts to achieve a more emotionally balanced life.

Acronyms such as MEDDSS provides common shared therapeutic language references, to make it easier to distill difficult life areas into a therapeutic focus. "Have you done your MEDDSS today?" is all the therapist needs to ask to convey a set of practices that need attention for good self-care.

In the following TIPS in this chapter, you are introduced to more of the DBT acronyms. Embracing the DBT model is really like learning a new vocabulary!

TIP #49

Non-DBT Acronyms Are All Around!

DBT is known for its use of acronyms, but acronyms are certainly not just limited to DBT. If you familiarize yourself with using acronyms in the DBT framework, you will quickly see that we use non-DBT acronyms every day. For example, most people learned the musical scale with acronyms. In school we were taught, *All Good Boys Deserve Fudge* and *FACE* to remember the musical staffs.

Can you think of some common acronyms?

_____

_____

_____

Below are some well-known acronyms that are so well established that the acronyms themselves are generally more popular than the phrases that they stand for.

ATM: Automated Teller Machine

ADD: Attention Deficit Disorder

AIDS: Acquired Immune Deficiency Syndrome

EPCOT: Experimental Prototype Community of Tomorrow

FEMA: Federal Emergency Management Agency

24/7: All the time, 24 hours a day, 7 days a week

AA: Alcoholics Anonymous

ASAP: As Soon as Possible

FYI: For Your Information

B.C.: Before Christ

A.D.: Anno Domini, year of the Lord

Here are some of my own examples:

LIFE: Loving Is For Everyone is what LIFE is all about!

PEACE: Positive Energy Always Creates Excellence!

My personal favorite? *TIPS* of course!

Treatment Ideas and Practical Strategies and Theory, Implementation and Processing

Now it's your turn to make your own acronyms!

What are some skills or concepts that are important to you? Write them down. Can you form them into an acronym?

To get you started, here are some ideas:

YES: You Expect Success! *Can you think of another?*

Y

E

S

WAIT: Why Am I Troubled? *Can you think of another?*

W

A

I

T

LIVE: Live in Victory Each Day! *Can you think of another?*

L

I

V

E

Now your turn. Think of one of your favorite words. Then think of an acronym for it, using each letter to represent a word or phrase that reflects the general meaning of the word.

_____

_____

_____

_____

TIP #51

DBT Fast Facts

Dialectical Behavior Therapy was originated by Dr. Marsha Linehan at the University of Washington. DBT grew out of her research involving treatment of suicidal patients, primarily either diagnosed or having characteristics of those with Borderline Personality Disorder.

1. Recognizing the difficulty of borderlines and other suicidal and high-risk patients to cope with their intense emotions and difficulty in controlling their impulses, Linehan developed a series of life skills coping strategies using various change-based and acceptance-based concepts.

2. Linehan's website, BehavioralTech.org, offers many resources including free downloadable handouts and worksheets from the DBT model.

3. The ideal DBT model includes both individual and group psychotherapy. The group therapy is psychosocial and psycho-educational in orientation, and teaches practical life skills in a sequential basis outlined in Linehan's book for therapists, *Cognitive-Behavioral Treatment of Borderline Personality Disorder*. In her book, she outlines the eight-session DBT group framework which has certain topics each time that are covered, and clients can benefit from more than one round of this group to keep having certain skills reinforced.

4. DBT is a behavioral approach which addresses the *dialectics* in everyday life. *Dialectics* stands for things that appear to be in conflict, or apparently *opposite*, addressing the existence of the many paradoxes in life, with common conflicting emotions and thoughts we all experience. Although seemingly opposite, there are kernels of truth in almost anything, so it encourages seeing things in shades of gray, not extreme in black and white.

5. DBT exercises help the client balance and combine life's dialectics and strive for a life balance instead of seeing things in black and white. Rather, making peace with life's apparent conflicts helps us become more balanced and accepting of the gamut of emotions and thoughts that we experience.

6. DBT has been a meshing of Eastern and Western psychological approaches. Acceptance-based skills are joined with change-based skills.

7. Change-based skills include Emotional Regulation and Interpersonal Effectiveness.

8. Acceptance-based skills include Mindfulness and Distress Tolerance.

9. The DBT model ideally includes individual counseling each week, one psycho-educational group session, a phone call between sessions, peer supervision and weekly support group to help clinicians support one another working with highly challenging individuals.

10. DBT frequently uses acronyms to help remember important elements of the key concepts of life skills.

11. Linehan believed that personality predisposition plus environmental and family invalidation are the key factors in the development of a Borderline Personality.

12. In DBT's second wave, Linehan's model serves as a foundation for innovative practitioners to add new activities in all her four content areas. The intention is to increase the tools therapists can use to be flexible in their treatment, within the model of the four content areas.

TIP #52

Acceptance Is the Key!
Mindfulness and Distress Tolerance

THEORY: Marsha Linehan's focus on mindfulness grew out of her dissatisfaction with Cognitive Behavior Therapy's focus on change at the expense of unconditional acceptance and validation of the individual. Her interest in non-traditional Eastern approaches arose from her own study of Zen, as a practitioner as well as a Zen teacher. She believed that the main drawback of CBT's focus was on the disregard for validation and acceptance. For the high risk client, particularly the suicidal and Borderline Personality, Linehan believed there needed to be much more focus on validating the individual and teaching clients to be less judgmental of themselves. Since she believed that suicidal and borderline clients generally lack sufficient validation in their upbringing, treatment needed to focus on providing the validation as part of their healing.

Linehan's focus on acceptance-based skills includes the two broad categories of *mindfulness* and *distress tolerance*. Linehan saw a need for such high risk clients to develop mindfulness strategies to control destructive impulses and drama-ridden thoughts and feelings. Acceptance is often called *radical acceptance* in the DBT model, which addresses the need not only for the therapist to validate the client but more importantly for the client to develop skills for their own self-validation and skill building strategies – without conditions.

IMPLEMENTATION: The following worksheets are either from the classic DBT model or part of the *second wave* of DBT. They are all skills to be practiced regularly. The skills can be on a DBT diary card which basically mentions a list of skills (many are acronyms) cross referenced with the days of the week, and the client is to circle or put a check for each day that this certain skill was practiced.

PROCESSING: These sample sheets provide a glimpse of the two areas of acceptance strategies in the DBT model, though there are many variations and techniques that are beyond the scope of this workbook. They are informational for you as the practitioner, for your client as part of their education, and then some for skill building practice.

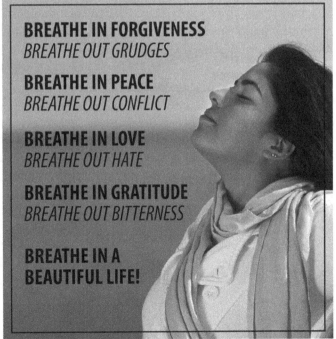

BREATHE IN FORGIVENESS
BREATHE OUT GRUDGES

BREATHE IN PEACE
BREATHE OUT CONFLICT

BREATHE IN LOVE
BREATHE OUT HATE

BREATHE IN GRATITUDE
BREATHE OUT BITTERNESS

BREATHE IN A
BEAUTIFUL LIFE!

TIP #53
Teaching Your Clients to Observe Mindfully

THEORY: Observing non-judgmentally is a challenge for all of us, but particularly those who have a hard time controlling their emotionality and impulses. Linehan makes the point that mindfully observing is non-judgmental without interpretations. By being mindful under times of distress, a person will be less carried away by their own subjective interpretations, and thus they will be less caught up in personalized emotional distress. By being able to observe mindfully, they would be more likely to stay calm.

IMPLEMENTATION: For example, looking at your hand, what do you see? If you mindfully observe, you would say "five fingers, ring on one finger" and if you were to judgmentally observe, the response would be more like "dry looking, wrinkly fingers, looking old."

Another example that I like to do with clients is to wrinkle up my face. I then ask them what they see. Those who are using judgmental terms would say things like, *"you look mad"* or *"you look worried."* I explain to them that they are now interpreting my gestures rather than mindfully observing and describing.

I then explain that a mindful description would be *"your nose is wrinkled, your eyebrows are furrowed, your lips turned down."*

Observing mindfully is being descriptive with no commentary in the NOW, rather than comparing how something differs from previously.

Of course, your client will experience judgmental thoughts, but the idea is to learn mindfulness skills so they can catch when they put themselves or others down with evaluations. Suggest to them to watch these judgmental thoughts float by, observe them but do not allow them to overpower you. Let them come and go and you watch them like a movie!

PROCESSING: If your client practices these mindfulness skills when they are not under duress, they will be more likely to stay calm and focus more on observing rather than judging during more stressful times.

Teaching our clients to stay in the *here and now* and to be more accepting of their lives without expecting that things should go their way is an acceptance practice that is not easy for most. Practicing mindfulness exercises, especially accompanied by relaxation techniques such as deep breathing and progressive relaxation of their body, help clients develop more acceptance of the things in life they cannot control.

TIP #54

Mindfulness Mnemonic: ONE MIND

One of the most fundamental acronyms for mindfulness in DBT is ONE MIND, originated by one of the foremost DBT experts, Thomas Marra, Ph.D. This mindfulness skill is focused on helping people to live in the moment, in the *HERE and NOW.*

He uses a mnemonic, which is similar to an acronym, but each letter of the word does not necessarily start at the beginning of the phrase.

When you practice ONE MIND, you are focusing on:

O: One thing at a time

N: Being in the here and Now

E: Attend to the Environment

M: Be attentive to the Moment

I: Increase your five senses

N: Take a Non-judgmental stance

D: Describe what you experience without interpretation

If you practice ONE MIND, you are working on taking an objective, non-judgmental stance in which you observe and describe what is going on around you without interpretations of yourself or others. You are taking in everything with all five senses, and you are feeling fully engaged in the experience.

The more you practice the meditative experience of ONE MIND, the more accepting you will be with what happens in your life, and the more you will be open to living fully in the present.

How about you? How about consciously committing to practice ONE MIND for even 5 minutes a day? Your mind will likely wander, but just watch it like a movie and bring it back.

When you are mindful, you are more present-focused and savor your everyday mundane experiences such as eating, walking, working, washing dishes, etc. with heightened awareness of the present. The more you practice ONE MIND, the more you will be *HERE* and not *OUT THERE!*

TIP #55

Turtling as a Mindfulness Skill

Cathy Moonshine, Ph.D., has a great metaphor for mindfulness self-care: **"Turtling."** Using the metaphor of a turtle, Moonshine finds many similarities between mindfulness strategies and turtling.

- She uses the analogy of how the turtles right themselves back up when they are turned over.
- They have shells to protect themselves.
- They proceed cautiously and intentionally.
- They are always "self-righting."
- They are adaptive – they adapt to land and sea.

In *Dialectical Behavior Therapy: Volume II*, Moonshine uses the metaphor of turtles for healthy self-care skills. For example, when we let things "roll off our backs" we are being accepting and showing non-judgmental mindfulness.

1. Using the concept of turtling, how do you protect yourself?

_____

2. How do you or can you proceed cautiously especially in high stress situations?

_____

3. Turtles protect themselves not only by their shell but they do snap when attacked – how do you stand up for yourself?

_____

4. What are your behaviors when you protect yourself? Do you withdraw like a turtle?

_____

5. Can you think of any ideas about turtling?

_____

TIP #56

Distress Tolerance - The Other Acceptance Based Skill

How do you tolerate frustration?

Does your stress manage you or do you manage your stress?

We all have in our power the ability to soothe ourselves, even in the most stressful and frustrating times. Distress tolerance is in the acceptance content area of DBT, and has as its focus the ability to tolerate distress and frustration so you will be able to control your impulses in dealing with your frustration and anger.

By being accepting, mindful and non-judgmental, you will be able to manage your emotions and modulate them. That way, you'll be more apt to manage your stress rather than carry it!

There are specific strategies to help tolerate distress, and a few are highlighted below. Most are from Linehan's original classic model, with a couple from the newer wave of innovative DBT activities.

Self-Soothe Kit – Both Scott Spradlin (*Don't Let Your Emotions Ruin Your Life*) and Cathy Moonshine (*DBT Workbook: Volume II*) suggest assembling a kit for self-soothing. In the kit might be magazine clippings of soothing places, pictures of pets, friends and family or those in the media, and other "good luck" or sentimental items that provide comfort. Developing a box filled with soothing items, even a 'virtual' file on the computer, can be very comforting in times of stress.

Regardless of whether it is a tangible self-soothing kit or a virtual one on your computer, the important thing is that when you are under stress, you have the soothing triggers that help keep you grounded.

****

Radical Acceptance: This means to completely and unconditionally accept what you have no control over. It is a skill in which you refocus your attention on what you can control, rather than on what you can't – including other people! When you intentionally focus on *radical acceptance,* you are empowering yourself to accept life as it is, not what you expect it to be.

****

Bridge Burning (BB): In his *DBT Skills Training Manual,* Lane Pederson suggests a bridge burning activity that can be used to help clients focus on burning their bridges of destructive behaviors. Removing alcohol and drugs from their home, putting distance between them and the people who encourage dysfunctional choices, cutting up credit cards if they are recklessly used, deleting phone numbers of people associated with your drug use, staying away from bars and locations where drugs and alcohol are consumed, and removing any objects like razors used for self-injury, are all some examples of bridge burning activities.

****

Half Smile: No matter how you feel, if you focus on managing even a *half smile* you will likely feel less stressed and focus on what in your life gives you something to smile about. Even when you are upset, find something that you are happy about and balance out your negative feelings with positive ones. You will then be able to at least half smile. This intention to think of something good to balance out the unpleasant will help dissolve the tension/stress you are feeling. Half smiles are also reinforcing. The more you smile at people around you, the more they smile back at you! Use a half smile consciously on a regular basis and you will likely feel better!

It's a fact: *If you love life, life will love you back!*

Linehan's use of the acronym IMPROVE focuses on ways to develop mindfulness. With enough practice, the goal is that during stressful times, your mindfulness skills will help you cope. Make IMPROVE part of an everyday routine!

For each of the 7 points, write a sentence on how you can personalize IMPROVE for yourself.

Imagery: Use imagery to visualize a peaceful scene, use guided imagery, relaxation CDs, and make it a part of your everyday routine.

_____

Meaning: Find meaning in each experience you have. Everything can help you grow if you let it! Find a purpose to your life.

_____

Prayer: Ask help from a higher spiritual power, or even others. There is hope!

_____

Relaxation: Take a breath! Doing slow breathing will calm you down and increase oxygen!

_____

One-Mindfully: Focus on taking one step at a time, one thing at a time.

_____

Vacation: Take time for yourself by taking a walk or calling a friend, even for a couple minutes.

_____

Encouragement: Be your own cheerleader. Say nice things to yourself!

_____

TIP #58

Self-Soothe with Your Senses

Linehan suggests using your five senses to develop your relaxation rituals so that in times of stress you will use your five senses to calm yourself.

How can you self-soothe with your five senses in times of stress?

SIGHT: Examples of how to be mindful through sight is finding pleasing objects, scenes of nature, people or animals to look at (even a picture) or having a collage or drawing of your favorite things you can bring out that trigger peaceful emotions. Your own personal collage can serve as a wonderful reminder of sights of hope, peace or love, for example. Even a computer screen saver could be a place for a soothing sight.

What sights are self-soothing to you?

SOUND: Listening to a waterfall on your computer or outside, listening to music or comforting sounds can help immerse you in the moment. The more mindful you are, the more you might be able to hear different things than you heard before, focusing on being more mindful of the music!

What sounds are soothing to you?

TOUCH: Petting an animal, stroking a loved one, covering yourself with a fleece blanket or sweatshirt, are all examples of using touch for mindful immersion.

What can you touch that is soothing to you?

TASTE: All too often we eat and are not focused on what we are eating. Many of us do not eat slowly and savor each bite. Having a small raisin, sip of water, or bite of food and savoring it will help you develop mindfulness skills through taste.

What can you taste that is soothing to you?

SMELL: Smells of nature, scented candles, aromas, incense, and cologne are all examples of smells that can create a path to mindful immersion. Baked goods hot from the oven are also nice!

What can you smell that is soothing to you?

TIP #59

The Change-Based Skills of Emotional Regulation

THEORY: Whereas the acceptance-based strategies were more geared towards coping with a better emotional perspective on the inside, DBT's change-based skills are focused on behavioral strategies for outward change.

Thus, after the acceptance-based skills in the DBT model have been established, the focus goes on to encompass change-based skills. Emotional regulation follows from the ability to tolerate distress, and emotional regulation activities are designed to help control and alter behavioral reactions. Once the acceptance-based skills create a calmer mind, then there is increased readiness for learning behavioral strategies to improve interpersonal effectiveness. Behavioral skills to better control impulses become the focus on increasing your client's ability to handle life's upheavals. Stress management and assertiveness training groups have been around since the 1970s, and fit very well into the Interpersonal skills content area. These groups focus on tactful self-expression with confidence while respecting the rights of others. DBT borrows many valuable resources from assertive training and stress management programs with a skill building focus and a practical "hands on" orientation which dovetail very nicely with DBT's change-based skill focus.

IMPLEMENTATION: In the following section, I have included Linehan's classic work as well as innovative DBT strategies from DBT's *new wave* of practitioners for personal and interpersonal coping skills with a heavy emphasis on "doing." All handouts and worksheets are self-explanatory and certainly can be used by any practitioner who is looking for hands-on ideas and practical strategies to use with individuals and groups.

PROCESSING: When discussing strategies with your client, reinforce the notion that the best time to practice behavioral skills is when they are not in a crisis. If your clients learn and practice skills when they are not under duress, they will be more likely able to use them when they are in more stressful situations. It gives them a chance to form better habits to use in challenging times. Otherwise, it would be like teaching someone to swim when they're drowning – that it is certainly not the time to give swimming lessons!

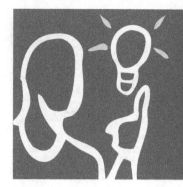

TIP #60

Emotional Regulation Strategies Sampler

Here are a few samples of the types of activities and visualizations with the DBT focus on Emotional Regulation. As usual in DBT, acronyms and metaphors are heavily used to make the ideas for Emotional Regulation easy to remember and user-friendly. A nice exercise with clients is to have them make up their own acronyms individually or as a group. For example, after giving the examples below, if you want an activity to create acronyms in group intervention, have the participants write their own and share with the group. Or for a more structured activity, write some words that are soothing on a flip chart, such as CALM, SOOTHE, PEACE, LOVE, HELP, HEALTH, YES, JOY and have the group use those. A fun idea for a group activity is to find a word that sums up your focus of the day and leave time at the end of the session to make an acronym for that topic word, then group participants can have a handy way to keep in mind some main points of your session.

MEDDSS: The acronym, **MEDDSS**, has already been outlined in the chapter introduction. **MEDDSS** stands for the areas of self-care that need attention every day.

> **M**astery **E**xercise   **D**iet **D**rugs (prescription)   **S**leep **S**pirituality

****

Ride the Wave: Psychologist Cathy Moonshine uses the metaphor of the ocean tides as a visualization for emotions that we experience. Sometimes the emotions build up into strong waves and other times the tides change and they weaken. You can either be crushed by the waves, or ride the waves. Using this metaphor, we can keep in mind that life is like changing tides, and we can either surf or be knocked down by them. It's all about balance! This metaphor is a great visualization for clients who are trying to build more self-mastery for the changing tides in their lives.

****

Psychologist Thomas Marra offers the acronym of **TRUST** to help individuals strengthen their coping skills.

> **T**rust Myself
>
> **R**edirect my impulses and urges
>
> **U**se my skills
>
> **S**ense my face, muscles, voice and posture
>
> **T**ame my emotions and impulses

****

Can you think of your own <u>metaphor</u> that represents emotional regulation?

_____

Can you think of your own <u>acronym</u> that represents emotional regulation?

_____

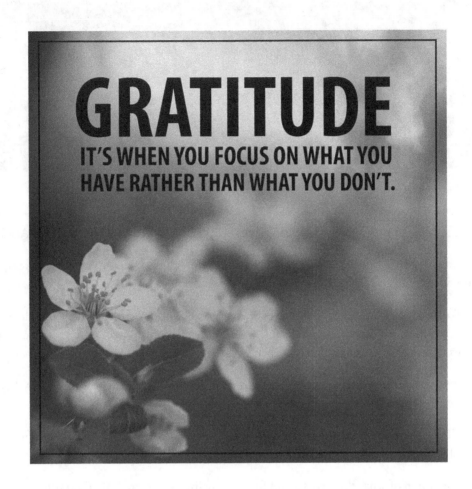

TIP #61

Learning the DBT ABCs

We learned the ABCs of Cognitive Therapy in the previous chapter. Now we can learn the **DBT ABCs!**

The acronym **ABC** is Linehan's classic acronym for reminding individuals, who are trying to strengthen their coping skills, of three basic ideas:

Accumulate Positives: Keep in mind the positives in your life. Have your client gather examples of good things that have happened to them, so that under stress and when things look bleak, your client will keep in mind the very positive things that they have accumulated in their lives.

Build Mastery: This reminds individuals to build on their accomplishments, realizing what they are good at and what they have mastered in their lives. Have clients identify skills that they are good at.

Cope Ahead: This is to remind clients of the coping strategies they developed. Since life often does not go as we plan, coping skills need to be developed to help cope with whatever comes our way.

After reading the description of what the ABCs stand for, personalize your own ABC Emotional Regulation skills.

Accumulate Positives

_____

_____

Build Mastery

_____

_____

Cope Ahead

_____

_____

TIP #62

Think Dandelions and Lemonade to Regulate Your Emotions!

As previously stated, metaphors are widely used in the DBT model to help clients get unstuck from old habits and patterns. Metaphors elicit emotions and help people get unstuck from their old patterns of thinking. Psychologist Cathy Moonshine effectively uses the metaphors of dandelions and lemonade to help individuals with controlling their emotions.

****

Dandelions are weeds that represent problems in our lives. As people with gardens know, weeds are generally more resilient than the flowers themselves! She makes the point that if you think the dandelions need to go, you will never get rid of them. Weeds are weeds, after all! However, if you learn to manage them, you will be able to have dandelions co-exist with the beautiful flowers.

Moonshine uses the metaphor of dandelions for problems like addictions. To be in recovery means to constantly be weeding your garden! The attentiveness never can go away! Just think of those who attend AA meetings many years after they became sober. Using the metaphor, they are still weeding their garden!

What do dandelions represent to you in your life? What weeds, or problems, do you need to address and manage in your life?

_____

_____

How could this metaphor of the dandelions help you? What strategies could you do regularly to help you manage your life's dandelions?

_____

_____

****

Moonshine also uses the metaphor of making lemons into lemonade. Lemonade is the metaphor for turning weakness into strength.

What are the lemons in your life?

_____

How can you make your life's lemons into lemonade? What good can you make come out of them?

_____

TIP #63
Interpersonal Skill Building

THEORY: The Interpersonal Effectiveness module is the fourth content area of DBT – helping individuals develop good interpersonal connections and support. The importance of communication and relationships cannot be overemphasized, and even in this TIPS book I have allotted a whole chapter on interpersonal communication and assertiveness skills.

In this section, I will share a couple of the traditional DBT TIPS. Refer to chapter 6 for more resources on communication which would fit very well with the DBT psychosocial learning component.

In my counseling, as well as in my wellness speaking and training, teaching the hallmarks of Assertive Communication has been one of the topics that has made the most impact. So many people lack the knowledge of what good Assertive Communication is, and even to identify the hallmarks of Assertive, Non-Assertive and Aggressive Communication helps people have insight to their own communication and that of others. TIP 64 will give you a good basic outline as a starting point and chapter 7 is dedicated entirely to Interpersonal Communication. Especially in the area of communication, the information does little without practice. Knowing about it is different than actually understanding it, so role play is vital to make the points really effectively. It is one thing to think you know what assertive is, but once we role play, many people confuse the three types of behavior and need help to identify. Only by demonstrations and practice can people really incorporate these concepts.

IMPLEMENTATION: The DBT acronyms and worksheets are easy for your client to understand and provide a foundation for insight into the relationship building module of DBT. Practice with developing interpersonal skills is the key, as developing healthy interpersonal behaviors might take a lot of practice. Role play, also called behavioral rehearsal, can help clients practice interpersonal skills. In my favorite role play below, I have individuals read the canned lines of an insensitive friend who is chronically late to pick me up and in this role play I speak up to the friend. I express myself using a lot of aggressive "you" statements, reacting *in kind* to the insensitive "put downs" in their canned lines. Even after we distinguish the three types of behavior, prior to the role play, I am most often considered assertive as people think I am just "defending myself" to this rude, late person reading the canned lines. After each of the role plays, we break down the lines one by one (for example, I tell the person to *wear a watch*) and it is clear why both the canned lines and my lines are aggressive.

Meeting Scene *for canned role play*

Friend: I'm here–Are you ready to go?

Friend: Oh, I hadn't noticed the time!

Friend: You're much too sensitive – I'm only 10 minutes late! what's the big deal?

Friend: Come on, you're being petty. It's not such a big deal!

Friend: But really - you shouldn't feel that way!

Friend: Ok - I'll try to be on time next time.

When someone in the group reads the canned lines, I play the friend who was waiting and start off the exercise with communicating aggressively with "should" statements and rhetorical questions that are, by definition, aggressive. However, most people think it is assertive since I am not yelling or speaking loud. Some of the aggressive responses I start off with are as follows: *"Where were you all this time?" "You should be wearing a watch!" "How could you say that?" "Well, you're being petty!"* and *"You shouldn't tell me how I should feel!"* (in essence, double "should-ing" on my friend).

In a later role play having the same group member read the canned lines, I contrast my previous communication with assertive "I" statements, keeping the goal in mind only to express myself without attacking the other person. These "I" statements include *"I feel uncomfortable being late" "We miss some of the important announcements at the beginning of the meeting"* and *"I just wanted to let you know that next time if you are not here by 6:30, I will just meet you there."*

PROCESSING: Sometimes I have people take turns role playing to be assertive before I demonstrate, which always brings up very interesting comments and issues, as well as a lot of laughter! It's not as easy as it seems! Some people also like to ham it up, and this makes for a fun yet informative group session. Groups also have fun hamming up being non-assertive, after we do the role play scenario with aggressive and then assertive communication.

Using these handouts as springboards for group discussion can also be quite beneficial especially when accompanied by the role plays. Groups are a great way to try out and practice new behavior and to get immediate feedback. In the group, participants also get to share their homework with one another. They can talk about interpersonal challenges, their experiences, and brainstorm how they could best deal with challenges.

Many times they role play real life scenarios with one another to get practice and feedback–both are invaluable to incorporating the communication concepts.

TIP #64

The Three Communication Styles

Differentiating Between the Three Types of Communication

Non-Assertive Behavior	Assertive Behavior	Aggressive Behavior
GOAL		
Avoids conflict	Expresses feelings and thoughts	Controls - get others to change
Seeks approval, needs to "be liked"	Respects self and others	"Teaches" even if "student" is unwilling
"Keep the peace"	Makes compromises	Tries to "win"
Allows others to "take over"	Asks for a change	Micromanages others to change
BEHAVIORAL HALLMARKS		
Keeps things in	"I" statements	"You" statements
Indirect/beats around the bush	Direct	Tactlessly Direct
Denying own rights	Self-respecting	Disrespectful
People pleasing	Mutual concern	Cares more about being pleased
"Doormat"	Upright, strong	Bully-ish
Allows people to take advantage	Kind	Takes advantage
Has a hard time saying "no"	Can say "no" and set limits	Invades others boundaries
COMMON FEELINGS		
Anger build up	Even tempered	Angry, indignant
Hurt	Confident	Superior
Anxious	Calm	Righteous (maybe guilty later)
Depressed	Happy	Vengeful, blaming
Insecure, lack of confidence	Secure, confident	Overconfident
Feels inferior	Feels strong	Feels superior
REASONS		
Feels "helpful" and "nice"	Wants to "Spread the love"	Feels justified to control
Irrational thought blocks	Clear thinking	Irrational thought blocks
Overreacts from past issues	Present focused	Overreacts from past issues
Lacks assertive skills	Has assertive skills	Lacks assertive skills
Think they're "polite"	Polite but firm limits	They think they are assertive
Fearful	Secure	Prior non-assertive behavior erupts from being held in

Judith Belmont, MS (2013) • 127 More Amazing TIPS and TOOLS for the Therapeutic Toolbox: DBT, CBT and Beyond • www.belmontwellness.com • All rights reserved

TIP #65

What Is My Interpersonal Communication Style?

The handout describing the three types of communication is commonly used for anyone wanting to improve their communication skills and understand their interactions with others.

Reflecting on the three types of behavior, answer the following questions to sharpen your understanding of your communication style.

1. I generally consider my communication style _____. Explain.

2. How does my communication style differ if I am under stress:

    At work with co-workers?_____

    At work with clients or customers?_____

    At home with my family?_____

    With my friends?_____

3. Who is the one person with whom I have the most difficulty being assertive? Explain.

_____

4. What are ideas to improve my communication?

_____

5. Write down a situation in which you want to assert yourself.

_____

6. What is your goal?

_____

7. Ask yourself: Is this goal aggressive or assertive? How can you tell? If the goal is to change someone's mind or behavior it is aggressive, even if very well meaning. If it is meant only to express yourself, then it is assertive!

_____

TIP #66

Have You Practiced Your DEAR MAN Today?

Perhaps one of the most popular acronyms in DBT and the most widely practiced is DEAR MAN. This concept is used to depict the skills necessary to relate to others and develop skills for building strong relationships. Role playing is a great way to practice your interpersonal skills using DEAR MAN as a guide, either with one other person or in a group setting.

For each of the seven topics, write an example that relates to you.

Describe the situation, non-judgmentally and objectively.

_____

Express your thoughts and feelings tactfully.

_____

Assert your wants and wishes clearly.

_____

Reinforce others who respond positively by also being positive. Express appreciation.

_____

Mindfully present, without expectations for others to be different. Accept the reaction of others rather than judge it!

_____

Appear confident; do not raise your voice or talk in a way that demeans you.

_____

Negotiate with others; compromise, instead of trying to get your way.

_____

TIP #67

What Did You GIVE?

GIVE is another acronym in the foundation of Linehan's model of Interpersonal Effectiveness.

This acronym helps those learning DBT to be:

Gentle: Be courteous and kind without attacks or threats.

Interested: Show interest in talking as well as listening to what the other person says.

Validate: Validate the thoughts and wishes of other people as worthwhile.

Easy Manner: Use humor and light heartedness – not so serious and tense!

For each of the 4 topics, fill out your own personalized '*GIVE*' worksheet. How would these concepts fit into your life?

Gentle

_____

Interested

_____

Validate

_____

Easy Manner

_____

Since DBT uses so many acronyms as well as metaphors, can you think of a <u>metaphor</u> for GIVE?

G

_____

I

_____

V

_____

E

_____

TIP #68
Diary Keeping a la DBT

THEORY: There is no shortage of DBT cards on the internet to help individuals track their progress and attentiveness to the various skills they learn in the DBT counseling model.

Below is not an official DBT card, but a sample of one of the types of cards you might see used.

IMPLEMENTATION: One of the cornerstones of DBT is diary keeping. It is a short and simple grid that you can use in a variety of ways depending on the skills being addressed. The typical diary card has the skills to work on along the left hand side, and then each day of the week across the top, and therefore your client can keep a record of when each skill is used.

There are many DBT cards to download online from various sites. My personal favorite is dbtselfhelp.com. There are even apps for your smart phone to keep a DBT diary!

You can simply use a calendar, even on your computer, to track what skills you are working on that day. For example, if you focus on Mindfulness and ONE MIND, you would check off the item or write that down on the day you focused on it, to help you reinforce the skills learned in the DBT model. I have provided only a small sample here due to copyright.

PROCESSING: Diary cards can be processed in both individual and group sessions, and serve as a very good way to see how motivated your client is to work on skills during the week, and can help you and your client track their progress.

SKILL	MONDAY	TUESDAY	WEDNESDAY	THURSDAY	FRIDAY	SATURDAY	SUNDAY
MEDDSS	•		•		•	•	
DEAR MAN			•	•			•
IMPROVE	•			•		•	
ONE MIND		•		•			
GIVE			•		•	•	

5

**Positive
Psychology**

TIPS 69–78

TIP #69

Staying Positive with Positive Psychology

THEORY: Positive Psychology, with its focus on happiness and well-being, is a relatively new field, although the roots go way back centuries ago. Socrates and Plato focused on happiness and self-knowledge as essential life pursuits. The religion of Judaism was founded on the idea that happiness is gained through a moral and religious life. The Declaration of Independence was founded on the premise that all people had *"unalienable Rights, that among these are Life, Liberty and the pursuit of Happiness."*

The roots of the actual field called Positive Psychology were much more recent, dating back to the movement of Humanistic Psychology in the 20th century, spearheaded by Carl Rogers and Abraham Maslow. Humanistic Psychology veered off from the typical study of mental illness, shifting the focus from Psychopathology to Self-Actualization and Personal Growth. In the last 20 years, Martin Seligman provided the foundation of the mental health movement called Positive Psychology, with his focus on optimism, happiness, well-being and "flourishing." His book titles reveal this focus: *Learned Optimism: How to Change Your Mind and Your Life; Flourish: A Visionary New Understanding of Happiness and Well-Being;* and *Authentic Happiness: Using the New Positive Psychology to Realize Your Potential for Lasting Fulfillment.* In the graduate program he founded at the University of Pennsylvania, he offers the first advanced program in Positive Psychology called the Master of Applied Positive Psychology (MAPP). Areas of gratefulness, kindness, mindfulness, and resiliency are examples of Positive Psychology. I have also included two self-tests with permission from another one of the pioneers of Positive Psychology, Ed Diener with his associates, on life satisfaction and flourishing.

IMPLEMENTATION: The field of Positive Psychology studies how and why people are happy and how people can increase wellness in their lives. The study and practice of well-being and life satisfaction has many offshoots. In the following section, there are some handouts and accompanying worksheets for improving wellness. I have found these helpful with not only working with clients, but in writing guest blog posts on personal development and wellness sites. I enjoy reaching a wider audience as part of my work, and guest blogging provides this opportunity (more about this in the social media chapter). Some of these handouts and worksheets are in fact adapted from some of my most popular posts that were shared by thousands of self-help aficionados.

This chapter is a brief introduction to Positive Psychology, and consists mostly of handouts on various TIPS for leading a happier, more fulfilling life. However, the influence of this field is so prominent in modern culture and in the media, that many characteristic TIPS of this field are in other areas of this book, especially the last two chapters concerning *Social Media* and *Therapist in Your Back Pocket* (for people on the go). You will also find topics pertaining to Positive Psychology like no other psychological discipline all over the media, with society's current preoccupation with health, wellness and happiness.

PROCESSING: Each of these self-empowering and positive handouts and worksheets depicts areas of wellness, such as gratefulness and happiness. They can be best used as self-help assignments between sessions, and are great springboards for discussion and processing in individual and group sessions. In group sessions, taking turns reading aloud one of the handouts and then picking a favorite TIP can set the stage for a productive and positive discussion. Positive Psychology is less about coping skills and more about transforming and actualizing yourself.

To sum up in a phrase, *thriving, and not just surviving,* is the focus of Positive Psychology.

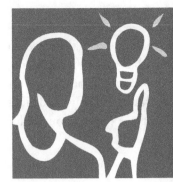

TIP #70

Focusing on Positivity

THEORY: With the popularity of Positive Psychology, the focus of positivity has become a cornerstone of current psychotherapeutic approaches. Positivity focuses on positive emotions and wellness rather than focusing on negative emotions, pathology and personality deficits. As clients seek treatment due to life issues, helping them understand the importance of gratitude, joy, fun, and general emotional wellness in their healing will help clients more readily find positive solutions to their problems.

IMPLEMENTATION: You can help clients empower themselves by offering resources and TIPS in the area of Positive Psychology. These are some of the main topics within the Positive Psychology field:

- Gratefulness
- Wellness
- Positive thinking
- Happiness
- Inspiration
- Hope
- Success
- Self-empowerment
- Inner peace
- Law of Attraction
- Spirituality
- Love

Online resources are plentiful. Here are just a few of my favorite examples: (I expand on these in my social media section.)

Facebook: There are many sites with pictorial quotes to inspire and motivate. Therapists, as well as the general public, have community pages that are separate from a personal Facebook account, where inspiring pictures and quotes are posted and shared on other pages.

Blog Sites: Blogs for personal growth and development are numerous and welcome interaction through comments and guest postings.

Pinterest: This popular social media site is a great vehicle for posting blogs and pictorial inspirations. Many postings are traded and shared online.

PROCESSING: The focus on positivity will help you motivate and inspire your clients to see solutions in their lives in place of their problems. I commonly refer my clients to online sites so that they can read positive blog posts I recommend, and follow positive sites that offer pictorial inspirations and quotes like my own. I have a separate "business" page for this use and do not share my own personal Facebook site with clients. Having a web presence through various modalities increases your opportunity to promote your positive message, as well as offer your clients a place to get resources for inspiration and encouragement.

TIP #71

Ten Tips for Staying Positive – No Matter What!

Are you waiting for life events to turn out the way you want so that you can feel more positive about your life? Do you find yourself having pre-conditions to your sense of well-being, thinking that certain things must happen for you to be happier? Do you think there is no way that your life stresses can make you anything other than "stressed out" and that other people *just don't understand*? If your answer is "yes" to any of these questions, you might find yourself lingering in the land of negativity for too long!

The following are some tips to keep positive no matter what comes your way.

1. Positive people don't confuse quitting with letting go.

Instead of hanging on to ideas, beliefs, and even people that are no longer healthy for them, they trust their judgment to let go of negative forces in their lives.

2. Positive people don't just have a good day–they make a good day.

Waiting, hoping and wishing seldom have a place in the vocabulary of positive individuals. Rather, they use strong words that are *pro-active* and not *reactive*. Instead of being passive, positive people get involved in constructing their lives.

3. For the positive person, the past stays in the past.

Good and bad memories alike stay where they belong–in the past where they happened. They don't spend much time pining for the *good ol' days* because they are too busy making new memories now.

4. Positive people are grateful.

Positive people are grateful people. They do not focus on the potholes of their lives. They focus on the pot of gold that awaits them every day, with new smells, sights, feelings and experiences. They see life as a treasure chest full of wonder.

5. Rather than being stuck in their limitations, positive people are energized by their possibilities.

Optimistic people focus on what they can do, not what they can't do. They are not fooled into thinking that there is a perfect solution to every problem, and they are confident that there are many possibilities. They try new solutions to old problems.

6. Positive people do not let their fears interfere with their lives!

Positive people have observed that those who are defined and pulled back by their fears never really truly live a full life. While proceeding with appropriate caution, they do not let fear keep them from trying new things. They have faith they can get up when life knocks them down.

7. Positive people smile a lot!

When you feel positive on the inside it is like you are smiling from within and these smiles are contagious. Furthermore, the more that others are with positive people, the more they tend to smile too! Positive people don't take themselves so seriously!

8. People who are positive are great communicators.

They realize that assertive, confident communication is the key to healthy relationships. They avoid judgmental, angry interchanges, and do not let someone else's *blow up* give them a reason to react *in kind*. Rather, they express themselves with tact.

9. Positive people realize that if you live long enough, there are times for great pain and sadness.

One of the most common misperceptions about positive people is that to be positive, you must always be happy. This cannot be further from the truth. Being sad, angry and disappointed are all essential emotions in life. Positive people do not run from the gamut of emotions, they accept that all emotions are part of the healing process.

10. Positive people refuse to blame others and are not victims in life.

Positive people take responsibility for their reactions and do not blame others for "making them" feel a certain way. There is no place for holding grudges with a positive mindset. Forgiveness helps positive people become better, not bitter.

TIP #72

My Positivity Plan

1. After reading the Ten Tips for Staying Positive (TIP 71), how positive are you?

2. How many of the ten traits do you possess? What are they? _____
   _____

3. Pick your favorite tips that you would like to work on and explain how you can incorporate these ideas in your life.
   _____
   _____
   _____

4. What are some negative or unhealthy thoughts that interfere with your positivity?
   _____
   _____
   _____

5. What are your payoffs of negative thinking? _____
   _____

6. Think of a metaphor or visual image for a positive life. If it is small enough, carry it around with you or place it prominently in your car, purse, or desk. If it is not portable, draw or cut out a picture of the image from a magazine and keep it with you. Use it as a reminder to **Stay Positive**!

7. Make a plan of steps you can do every day to create a ritual of positivity (e.g., read inspirational quotes or affirmations each morning, go for a walk, or listen to soothing music).
   _____
   _____

TIP #73

Satisfaction with Life Scale

The following is a very well-regarded self-test in the files of Positive Psychology by Ed Diener & Associates.[3]

Below are five statements that you may agree or disagree with. Using the 1-7 scale below, indicate your agreement with each item by placing the appropriate number on the line preceding that item. Please be open and honest in your responding.

7 - Strongly agree

6 - Agree

5 - Slightly agree

4 - Neither agree nor disagree

3 - Slightly disagree

2 - Disagree

1 - Strongly disagree

_____ In most ways, my life is close to my ideal.

_____ The conditions of my life are excellent.

_____ I am satisfied with my life.

_____ So far I have gotten the important things I want in life.

_____ If I could live my life over, I would change almost nothing.

Add the number for the Total Score: _____

31 - 35 Extremely satisfied

26 - 30 Satisfied

21 - 25 Slightly satisfied

20   Neutral

15 - 19 Slightly dissatisfied

10 - 14 Dissatisfied

5 - 9   Extremely dissatisfied

---

[3]*Reprinted with Permission:* Ed Diener, Robert A. Emmons, Randy J. Larsen, and Sharon Griffin as noted in the 1985 article in the Journal of Personality Assessment. For more details on this test visit internal.psychology.illinois.edu/~ediener/SWLS.html

TIP #74

Self-Test: Are You Flourishing?

The following is another very well-regarded self-test in the field of Positive Psychology by Ed Diener and Associates.[4]

Flourishing Scale (FS)

Below are 8 statements with which you may agree or disagree. Using the 1–7 scale below, indicate your agreement with each item by indicating that response for each statement.

7 - Strongly agree

6 - Agree

5 - Slightly agree

4 - Mixed (neither agree nor disagree)

3 - Slightly disagree

2 - Disagree

1 - Strongly disagree

_____ I lead a purposeful and meaningful life.

_____ My social relationships are supportive and rewarding.

_____ I am engaged and interested in my daily activities.

_____ I actively contribute to the happiness and well-being of others.

_____ I am competent and capable in the activities that are important to me.

_____ I am a good person and live a good life.

_____ I am optimistic about my future.

_____ People respect me.

Total: _____

Scoring: The possible range of scores is from 8 (lowest possible) to 56 (highest personal well-being (PWB) possible). A high score represents a person with many psychological resources and strengths.

---

[4]Reprinted with Permission: Diener, E., Wirtz, D., Tov, W., Kim-Prieto, C., Choi, D., Oishi, S., & Biswas-Diener, R. (2009). *New measures of well-being: Flourishing and positive and negative feelings*. Social Indicators Research, 39, 247-266. © Copyright by Ed Diener and Robert Biswas-Diener, January 2009. For more information visit internal.psychology.illinois.edu/~ediener/SWLS.htm.

TIP #75
Ten Gratefulness Habits for a Happier Life

It is no secret that grateful people are happier people. Research findings, particularly in the rapidly emerging field of Positive Psychology have shown that gratefulness and life satisfaction go hand in hand. Those who tend to be more grateful rather than bitter are more positive and satisfied with their lives.

Here are ten habits of people with an *attitude of gratitude* mindset:

1. **Grateful people don't expect that life is going to give them everything they deserve.** They realize that good things do not always happen to good people, and they have given up the notion that life "owes them" anything more than it can offer. They know life is not fair and move on.

2. **They do not have preconditions to their happiness.** They do not think "If this happens…only then will I be happy." They understand happiness is not coming from the outside, but from within.

3. **People who are grateful have realized that you cannot have the rainbow without the rain.** They see rainy days as a normal part of life rather than an aberration, and learn from the rain rather than just wait for it to go away. Realizing you cannot have one without the other, they are grateful for it all! The thorns only make the rose seem sweeter!

4. **Grateful people have hope.** No matter what happens, hope is not lost. They take comfort in the fact that once the sun sets, it rises the next day. They have faith that there is more to life.

5. **Those who are steeped in bitterness and grudges have no space in their heart to be grateful.** Forgiving your spouse for mistakes made, forgiving your children for making choices that would not have been your own, and giving up grudges are all examples.

6. **People who are grateful know that a grateful attitude takes work.** Gratefulness does not always come naturally, especially in the most challenging times. They work at it! They might read affirmations, seek support from others, or seek counseling.

7. **Grateful people have healthy thinking habits.** They go by the motto, *"Think Straight–Feel Great!"* All-or-nothing/irrational thinking such as *"It's awful"* and *"I can't stand it"* is reserved for life-threatening circumstances, not everyday petty annoyances.

8. **Grateful people are flexible in their thinking.** People who think flexibly are at an advantage in life. They don't cling stubbornly to ways of thinking that do not work, and do not consider a shift in their attitude as meaning a personal defeat has occurred.

9. **People who love to learn tend to be grateful.** Grateful people focus more on the lessons they can get out of each situation rather than the disappointments. After all, life is a great teacher and teaches us things that no one else ever could.

10. **Grateful people define their self-worth by their determination and their dreams, not their regrets and disappointments.** A grateful mindset has no room for excessive self-recrimination. Thoughts shift to the goals they set to make things better now.

TIP #76

Start a Gratefulness Campaign in Your Life!

How about starting a gratefulness campaign in your own life? Start now by writing down at least ten things for which you are thankful.

1. _____

2. _____

3. _____

4. _____

5. _____

6. _____

7. _____

8. _____

9. _____

10. _____

Each day this week, bring this list with you and review it at least five times a day.

Every week make a new list of at least ten items and review it frequently.

What are current challenges that you are facing that you are not grateful for?

What blessings are there in these challenges? What can you learn from them? Remember that many times blessings become curses and curses become blessings!

TIP #77

Thankfulness is Good for Your Peace of Mind!

Thankful People are Happier People

Despite the enticing reasons for relegating thankfulness to one day of the year in the U.S., i.e. Thanksgiving, those who are more grateful in everyday life are happier people. Countless research findings, particularly in the rapidly emerging field of Positive Psychology, have shown that thankfulness and life satisfaction go hand in hand. For example, in his very gratifying book in the Positive Psychology field, Thanks! How the New Science of Gratitude Can Make You Happier (2008), UC Davis Psychology professor, Robert Emmons shows us that people who focus on being grateful are, as a whole, happier people. In his study with college students, he and his co-researcher McCullough found in a 10 week study that those students who wrote down five things each week that they were grateful for resulted in being 25 percent happier than those students who were simply asked to write down five things that happened each week. This study is just one of many that reveal that consciously practicing gratefulness makes us feel good!

Thankfulness is a choice – it is a gift you give to yourself!

If we choose to focus on what we are grateful for rather than what goes so wrong in our lives, we will get a great side effect to this attitude of gratitude. We will be happier! And if we are happier, people tend to be happier with us and we are happier with them! A win-win! So next time you think that life does not really deserve your gratitude, remember that it is not a matter of whether life deserves your gratitude – You deserve it!

Cultivate an attitude of gratitude!

The ability to be filled with gratitude has been found to be one of the main personality traits of personal well-being. Those who are filled with thankfulness and gratefulness for what is right in their lives tend to be happier and more resilient than those who focus on what is wrong or missing.

Ideas to help you remember to be more thankful in your life:
- It takes effort to focus on what is good in your life rather than what is not.
- If you focus on how you got a raw deal in life, you will find little room in your heart to be open to happiness.
- It's not a matter of whether life deserves your thankfulness – *you deserve it!*
- Being thankful is a choice. It is a gift you give to yourself.
- Be grateful as you sip your iced tea, take your next breath, and look in awe at a person that you really care about!

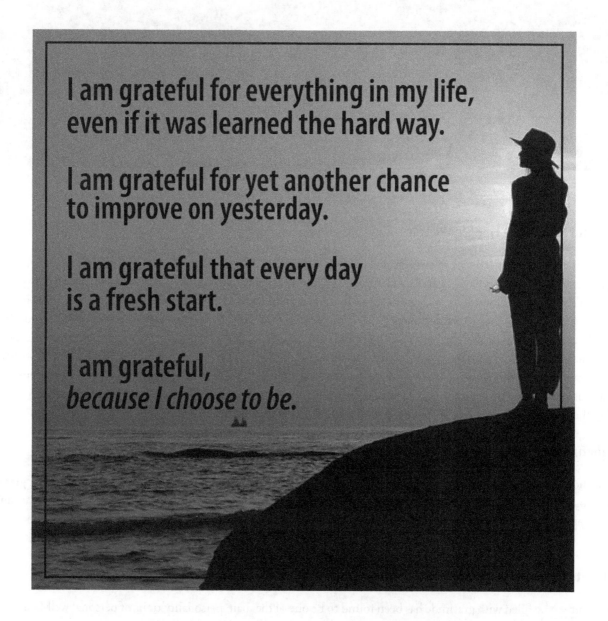

I am grateful for everything in my life, even if it was learned the hard way.

I am grateful for yet another chance to improve on yesterday.

I am grateful that every day is a fresh start.

I am grateful, *because I choose to be.*

TIP #78

Give Yourself a Second Chance Checklist

What's done is done.

We can't turn back the clock of life. Good or bad, right or wrong, it is done. It's over!

- Once the ingredients are mixed, we cannot separate them apart again.
- Once a word goes from our mouth, we cannot take it back.
- Once we do an action, we cannot choose another one in its place.
- Once wood is reduced to sawdust, you can't make it back into a board.
- Once Humpty Dumpty fell, all the king's horses and all the king's men couldn't put Humpty Dumpty together again!
- Once today arrives, it becomes too late to live in yesterday.
- The land of "woulda, coulda, shoulda" is not a place to live happily.

The good news is that there is an alternative to *I should have known better-itis*! Instead of wishing you had known better and kicking yourself that you didn't, how about giving yourself a second chance?

GIVE YOURSELF A SECOND CHANCE CHECKLIST:

- **Turn unproductive regrets into productive regrets.**
  Regrets are important in our life to help us self-correct. The key is to recover from and build on the sharp sting of regrets to look for the lessons learned and take comfort in the fact that these lessons make us wiser.

- **Take comfort in the fact that regrets help us develop empathy for others.**
  How would we ever develop real empathy if we never made a mistake or a wrong turn? It is regrets that keep us in check from being judgmental and arrogant. Thus, we become better people who, in turn, have more compassion and empathy for others. Empathy is considered to be one of the cornerstones of emotional intelligence.

- **The more wrong turns you made, in retrospect, help you increase the odds that your future choices will be more informed.**
  With so many lessons from mistakes or regrets, you will be in better shape moving forward. It can actually make it easier for us to be happier by living in today instead of yesterday.

- **Ask yourself–Did I do the best I could at the time? Undoubtedly, the answer will be "yes"!**
  People generally try their best, even if their best is not objectively healthy. Unhealthy people make unhealthy decisions and behave in an unhealthy way. People do not intentionally make self-defeating decisions. So consider it a noble effort to try your best, even if your best fell short and was misguided.

- **Moving from regrets is a ripe opportunity to work on the ability to forgive.**
  A lack of forgiveness for oneself or others is one of the most common reasons for depression, anxiety and interpersonal conflict. Thankfully, regrets give you the opportunity to self-correct, and to develop the ability to forgive–it brings them right to the surface to work on.

- **Use the broken pieces of unrealized dreams and disappointments as stepping stones towards a better future.**
  If you see shattered pieces of your life's dreams as stepping stones or as parts of a beautiful life mosaic, you can appreciate those broken remnants. All your disappointments, no matter how small or how large, can be part of something so beautiful and can pave the way for building a better tomorrow!

Conclusion

You cannot change what happened to you, but you can change *what you do* with what happened to you.

- So what are you waiting for? Give yourself a second chance. *You deserve it!*
- What do you need to give yourself a second chance?
- What regret can you turn from unproductive to productive?
- How could taking a second chance give you a fresh start?

REMEMBER – IT'S NEVER TOO LATE TO HAVE A SECOND CHANCE!

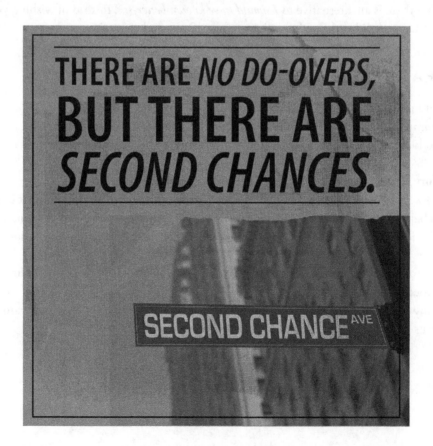

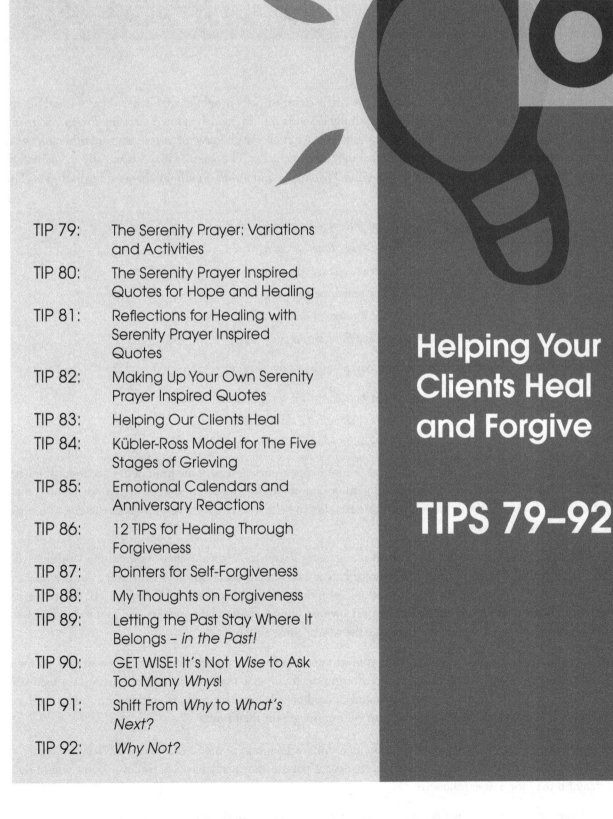

6

Helping Your Clients Heal and Forgive

TIPS 79–92

TIP #79

The Serenity Prayer: Variations and Activities

THEORY: In our work as mental health clinicians, we often strive to help people change what they can and accept what they can't. The depiction of this struggle is beautifully embodied in the widely quoted 'Serenity Prayer.' So many difficulties arise when this very simple message is not followed! After all, we all know of people who are miserable, who focus on trying to change things–and other people–that they cannot change. The Serenity Prayer is actually an adaptation of a prayer in a sermon delivered by prominent American Theologian and writer, Reinhold Niebuhr, in the 1930s. The first version actually went like this:

> *"God, give me grace to accept with serenity*
> *the things that cannot be changed,*
> *Courage to change the things*
> *which should be changed,*
> *and the Wisdom to distinguish*
> *the one from the other."*

It was later modified anonymously to what we know today, popularized by Alcoholics Anonymous and the 12 Step Program.

> *"God, grant me the serenity to accept the things I cannot change,*
> *The courage to change the things I can,*
> *And the wisdom to know the difference."*

I have often been struck with the notion that change cannot happen until at least some healing has occurred. If clients are not sufficiently healed to move on, they end up getting immobilized and end up unknowingly undermining their progress. This is why I started off this section with this exercise, to help your clients have a powerful exercise in healing before they embark on major changes.

IMPLEMENTATION: The following are take-offs of the Serenity Prayer to help your client heal, with a worksheet for them to fill out with their own version of the Serenity Prayer. Having clients create their own prayer with a relevant topic for personal healing, and using the structure of the Serenity Prayer and my versions in the next TIP, can be a great exercise both in individual and group treatment. For my own versions, I enjoy taking my own pictures or buying them from an online service to serve as a backdrop to make the words 'come alive.'

In a group situation, it can be meaningful to have your group members go around taking turns to read each of these Serenity Prayer take-offs aloud. After reading and reflecting on the ones I made up as a jumpstart, group members then make up their own. Provide heavy blank paper and colored pencils for them to draw up their own posters or have magazines, scissors and glue available so that they can cut out images for their poster.

PROCESS: Process with clients what makes it so difficult to follow the motto of the Serenity Prayer. What do they try to control in their lives that they really are powerless to change? What can they really have control over? How would their lives be different if the motto were followed?

TIP #80

The Serenity Prayer Inspired Quotes for Hope and Healing

These Serenity Prayer inspired posts are examples to share with clients of ways they can use the Prayer's general outline to make up their own takeoffs of the Prayer concerning issues relevant to them.

THE SELF-FORGIVENESS PRAYER

Lord grant me the ability to forgive myself for past stumbles and falls,

to correct what I can, and accept what I can't,

and the wisdom and courage to try again, this time a bit wiser.

THE PARENT'S PRAYER

Please grant me the ability to have dreams for my child to help guide them to grow,

To let go of those expectations that will stiffle their growth and wound their souls,

And to have the wisdom to know the difference.

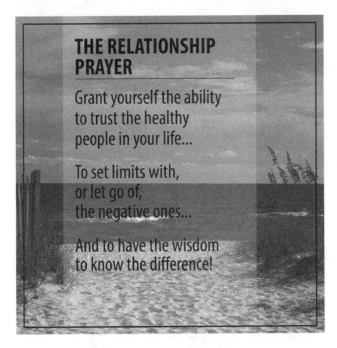

THE RELATIONSHIP PRAYER

Grant yourself the ability to trust the healthy people in your life...

To set limits with, or let go of, the negative ones...

And to have the wisdom to know the difference!

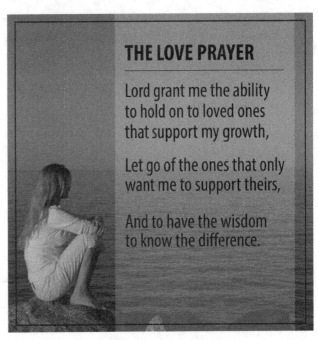

THE LOVE PRAYER

Lord grant me the ability to hold on to loved ones that support my growth,

Let go of the ones that only want me to support theirs,

And to have the wisdom to know the difference.

TIP #81

Reflections for Healing with Serenity Prayer Inspired Quotes

Which of the Serenity Prayer inspired quotes above is the most meaningful to you? Why?

_____

_____

_____

How can the Serenity Prayer, or any of the adaptations, help you heal?

_____

_____

What have you tried to change that you need to accept?

_____

_____

_____

What changes can you make in your life that are in your control?

_____

_____

_____

How does prayer and support from others help you with both changing what you can and accepting what you can't?

_____

_____

_____

How would your life be different if you were able to let go of what can't be changed?

_____

_____

_____

What feelings do these prayers trigger in you?

_____

_____

_____

 Judith Belmont, MS (2013) • 127 More Amazing TIPS and TOOLS for the Therapeutic Toolbox: DBT, CBT and Beyond • www.belmontwellness.com •

TIP #82

Making Up Your Own Serenity Prayer Inspired Quotes

To structure your own inspired prayer, consider the following:

1. What do you have a hard time accepting?

2. Do you find yourself struggling with trying to change things that are out of your control?

3. What do you need to accept that cannot be changed?

4. What are the things you are unsuccessfully trying to alter in your life, but don't have the inner peace and wisdom to let go of?

5. You might want to draw or cut out pictures from magazines that fit well with the area you are focusing on.

6. The end of the Serenity Prayer is "and the wisdom to know the difference." But of course, you can alter even this third line as in the example of The Self Forgiveness Prayer (above).

Now it's your turn! I offer two versions of the first line since some people would prefer to avoid religious references.

Grant Yourself _____ (First Line)

or

Lord, grant me _____ (First Line)

SECOND LINE _____ (Second Line)

And the wisdom to know the difference! (Third Line)

or

Make up your own third line! _____ (Third Line)

TIP #83
Helping Our Clients Heal

PROCESS: There are some things that we never get over—we just get through: traumas, hurt, tragedies, emotional or physical estrangement from loved ones, failures, disappointments, and life upheavals. Some seemingly insignificant losses, such as the loss of a friendship or a special loved one not having time for you or moving away, can also leave smaller scars than those of major upheavals.

Some scars are visible and can be seen on the outside, but many of our clients are in need of help because of the invisible scars within. The next few TIPS might be helpful resources in the healing process.

IMPLEMENTATION: Healing is variable and very individualized, although I have found Kubler-Ross's The Five Stages of Grieving very helpful in helping clients heal. When clients cannot understand why they are so angry at others, at themselves or at God, even way after their loss was experienced, I point to the handout The Five Stages of Grieving (TIP 84) to normalize their grief reaction. I always emphasize to my clients that grieving is not just about death– it is about the losses we go though in life, and of course we need to 'let go' to let other things in. If clients go from feeling like they have accepted a loss, then return back to anger and depression again, I refer to the sheet on grieving and explain that part of the grieving process is revisiting various stages as they heal. Healing does not go in a straight line, and it is not once-and-done forever. Situations, such as anniversaries of a loss, can be an example of a major trigger, and a handout and worksheet on that has been included in this section.

It seems very universal in the stages of grieving that healing through forgiveness—of self and others—is paramount. Those clients who cannot forgive, who harbor resentment, are the most treatment resistant. All too many people think that if you forgive, you let someone *off the hook*. Actually, when we forgive, we ourselves are off the hook of being trapped in the past. Forgiveness is not condoning–rather it is letting ourselves not be controlled by bitterness. Forgiveness is a key in the healing process, and actually this makes a great metaphor for forgiveness–the key to healing. We heal by forgiving that life was not more fair to us, that people were not more fair to us, and that we were not healthier at the time to behave differently.

PROCESSING: Forgiveness and healing is often a very central topic to many of our client's lives, and evokes a lot of emotion. I find The Five Stages of Grieving model by Kubler-Ross a great tool to normalize losses and to help make sense out of the complicated emotions that often go back and forth within ourselves as we try to move on after a gap is left in our lives.

TIP #84

Kübler-Ross Model for The Five Stages of Grieving

	Facing Mortality	Experiencing a Loss
Denial	I avoid facing the likelihood of my death. I cannot face mortality and I feel like I am invincible.	I ignore my hurt–I don't face it. I don't face things that are painful. I see things like I want to see them, and not as they are.
Anger	I am angry at life's unfairness. I am filled with resentment and can't forgive.	I blame others for hurting me. Others are responsible for my pain, I can't forgive. Anger consumes me.
Bargaining	I set up conditions to be fulfilled before I die. If I act or think certain ways, I can change and control the impossible.	I set up conditions to be fulfilled before I'm ready to forgive. If I act in a certain way, perhaps I can get others to change their mind or behaviors.
Depression	I blame myself for not fulfilling my dreams. I failed in my life–I didn't accomplish what I had hoped. I have much regret.	I blame myself for letting hurt destroy me. I failed and am ashamed of myself. Regrets consume me and I cannot live fully in the present.
Acceptance	I have prepared for my death and made requests of how my affairs should be handled. I've made peace with others and myself. I have come to terms with my mortality.	I look forward to growth. I can 'let go' and move on a bit wiser. I have hope for the future. I seek support for a new life. I accept my limitations.

TIP #85

Emotional Calendars and Anniversary Reactions

When a loss or trauma is experienced, such as a major upheaval, a break-up, or a death of a loved one, the anniversaries of that trauma have enormous power. Even if we feel we have grieved and "gotten over" a loss, other losses often trigger earlier losses as we go through life–especially during certain times of the year such as the holidays, our own birthdays, the birthdays of loved ones sorely missed, what would have been a wedding anniversary in the case of divorce or death, or the anniversary date of the loss itself. These trigger dates, called *anniversary reactions*, are significant markers on our emotional calendars that make our loss more conspicuous than in our day to day lives. It is normal to have feelings rise up again, even overwhelming grief and sadness, as you approach these dates of special significance. Unfortunately, most people do not even think of such 'anniversaries' as being risk factors, but if there is one thing we can learn from "psychological autopsies" of grief reactions involving self-harm and even suicide, it is that an anniversary of trauma can beget other trauma when a person hangs onto too much of the past.

If you anticipate these waves of feelings during these anniversary reactions on your emotional calendar, then you will be more prepared to cope with the emotional triggers of those reminders–even years later.

These are suggestions to cope with an anniversary reaction on your emotional calendar:

1. Expect these times to be difficult and do not judge your feelings. Accept them as normal and healthy.

2. Seek support from loved ones–don't go through it alone!

3. Express your feelings to those you trust–don't keep it in!

4. Prepare a ritual to focus on that helps you gain control and meaning in a time of grief (for example, going to the cemetery, lighting a candle, writing letters to your loved one each year).

5. Realize that new waves of grief are not to be avoided–they offer more opportunities to heal.

6. Heal your memories with forgiveness of yourself and others for mistakes and unfortunate choices that you made in the past.

7. Find new meaning and growth from the hurt.

8. Watch out for excessive use of drugs and alcohol. During certain times on your emotional calendar, using drugs–especially prescription medication such a sleeping pills and medications for anxiety, along with alcohol to ease the pain–will make things worse. Anticipate this common reaction and ask for support to prevent the likelihood that you will make unhealthy choices.

9. There is hope! Remind yourself that there is life after loss. It might help to write down ideas for new beginnings in your life and what you have to be grateful for. You might also want to write down how you have grown from the loss.

10. There are some things in life we will never really *get over*. Sometimes the best we can hope is to *get through*.

11. For those who have lost a loved one through suicide, be aware of what are called Anniversary Suicides. For instance, Mark Madoff, son of Ponzi-schemer, Bernie Madoff, committed suicide two years to the day after his father's arrest while his wife was away. Dana Plato's son committed suicide 11 years, almost to the day, of the *Different Strokes* star's suicide. Make sure there is plenty of support during the holidays when absences of loved ones are most keenly felt, as well as around the time of the tragic loss.

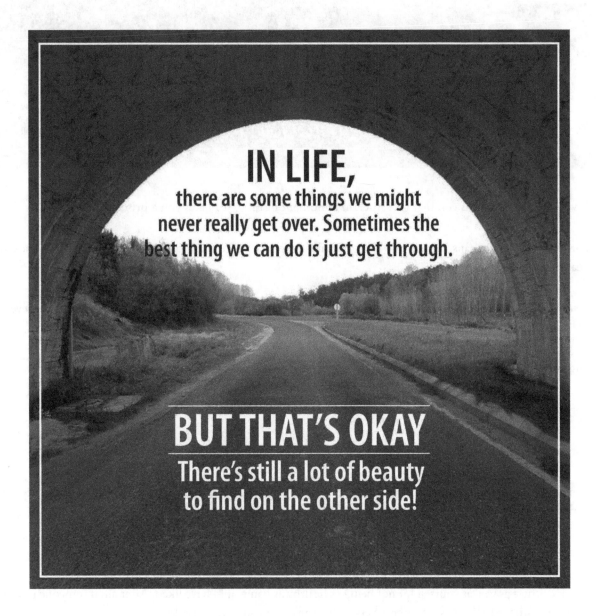

TIP #86

12 Tips for Healing Through Forgiveness

1. If you can't forgive, it is you that gets stuck in a moment of time. It makes you a prisoner of your past.

2. Forgiveness never means condoning–it means freeing yourself from the bitterness that holds you back from a healthier life.

3. Just because you forgive, it does not mean you stay around for more hurt. It is healthy to set limits and even avoid the transgressor forever, especially if there is abuse involved.

4. Forgiveness frees you from the burden of grudges–which holds you back from a more positive life.

5. Forgiveness helps you to let go of old wounds and helps you reclaim your life.

6. Forgiveness is about you–not the other person. It is about your own thoughts that are holding you back.

7. When you can't forgive, you are more likely to seek revenge and be vindictive, which brings out the negative and dark side in all of us.

8. Realize that some fences need repair and some fences cannot be fixed. Regardless, you can forgive anyway.

9. Forgive others as well as yourself for not being as healthy as you would have liked. After all, if someone is unhealthy they do not have healthiness to offer others. They can't give you what they don't have.

10. Forgiveness opens your heart, which allows you to heal from the hurt.

11. If you think they don't deserve your forgiveness, realize it is not about them - you deserve it!

12. The word FORGIVE can be broken down to two words–FOR and GIVE. Give yourself the ability to move forward.

TIP #87

Pointers for Self-Forgiveness

Self-forgiveness does not mean that you did not do something wrong, but it means that you allow yourself to learn from your mistakes and move forward. Too often people punish themselves for actions taken in the past, or can't forgive themselves for actions not taken.

Consider these points:

- If you are like most people, you did the best you could at the time.
- Do what you can now to make things right–let your regrets propel you into positive action, not keep you a prisoner of your past.
- If you need to apologize or make amends, do this now. Admitting fault is a sign of strength, not of weakness.
- Forgive yourself for not having the foresight that you now know in hindsight.
- It might be too late to change what happened, but it is not too late to change how you cope with what happened, and what you do about it now.
- In reality, most of our stumbles are not failures if we learn from them. They cause us to deepen and become wiser.
- You won't be able to be truly forgiving of others until you can forgive yourself.
- You can transform unproductive regret to productive regret. In productive regret, you build on lessons learned from the past and make new choices now.

Now it's your turn–can you add to these pointers?

REMEMBER: If you get stuck in regret and lack forgiveness, you will never set yourself free from being a prisoner of your past.

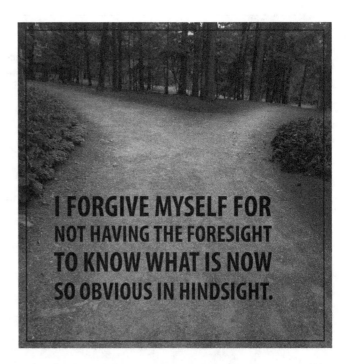

I FORGIVE MYSELF FOR NOT HAVING THE FORESIGHT TO KNOW WHAT IS NOW SO OBVIOUS IN HINDSIGHT.

TIP #88

My Thoughts on Forgiveness

What is the most difficult thing to I need forgive in others? In myself?

_____

What needs to happen for me to heal with forgiveness?

_____

What is holding me back? Am I keeping myself stuck in the past?

_____

How would my life be different if I were more forgiving?

_____

What do I need to do to take steps towards forgiveness?

_____

Psychologist Stephen Hayes uses a hook as a negative metaphor for lacking forgiveness—you are still on the hook and can't set yourself free from your offender and wherever your offender goes, there goes you!

What can be my positive metaphor for forgiveness?

_____

Below is my "forgiveness" plan. I will outline an action plan of what I can do to GIVE myself the ability to move FORward!

_____

_____

_____

_____

TIP #89

Letting the Past Stay Where It Belongs–in the Past!

Tal Ben-Shahar is a Harvard professor with one of the most popular classes on campus–a course on Happiness. He regards regret as undermining the potential for happiness. In his book, *Happier*, he writes,

> There are those who, stuck in the past, do not allow themselves to experience happiness in the present. They rehearse their unsatisfying histories...Always reliving the past, concerned with justifying their unhappiness, they forgo the potential for happiness in their lives.

Regret has its place though. If we did not regret at all, we would not have sufficient moral character to learn from our setbacks and improve on our behavior. In fact, Neal Roese, in his book *If Only*, claims that regret can be productive if you can learn from it rather than repeat the same mistakes over and over.

Instead of defining yourself in the past tense, how about turning unproductive regret into productive regret, spurring you on to make new choices with the wisdom gained?

Think of a regret that you have, and transform it into a productive regret. How? With these few simple questions:

1. What lessons have I learned about myself from my regret?

_____

2. What have I learned about others and life itself?

_____

3. What can I do now to build on what I have learned?

_____

4. Imagine your regret belongs to someone else. Would the regret seem as bad?

_____

5. Am I being too hard on myself?

_____

6. Think of at least one gift this regret has taught you.

_____

7. How has it helped me become a more compassionate and wiser person?

_____

TIP #90

GET WISE! It's Not Wise to Ask Too Many Whys!

"Why is he so shy?"

"Why didn't our relationship last?"

"Why can't I seem to get my life together?"

"Why am I so sensitive?"

"Why didn't my child turn out better?"

Although asking yourself "why" has its place so that we can learn from the past and be more aware going forward, the obsession that many of us have with why leads less to insights and more to preoccupation with a past that we might never figure out.

Although there is nothing wrong with occasionally indulging in this burning question, all too often the *whys* in our lives become an unending and persistent rumination rather than a quest for insight. The trouble is, we never really figure out definitively the whys in our lives, and we end up spending too much time focusing on the burning question rather than coping with it and learning to change now.

It is all too common for many people to get wrapped up in trying to make peace with past events, yet find that it can go only so far in unlocking the secrets of how to live better today. When we insist on finding conclusions, we end up having only more questions that start with why.

Perhaps there is some magical thinking that by discovering the truth, it will "make it all better." Yet the past never changes, and insight into the past does not automatically help us undo the effects of it.

In sum, focusing too much on the whys in our lives keeps us stuck in the past. Consider the following:

- The past never changes, so we likely remain stuck in the land of *whys*.
- Even if we uncover our life's *whys*, it does not mean they can be fixed.
- Rarely in life do we have "aha!" moments, when the past is totally figured out.
- Sometimes we just don't know why things happened. THEY JUST DID!
- Focusing on why gives you a good reason to stay in your old comfort zone. *Whys* can keep you a victim, making you likely to spend a life of blame.

So how about using your whys sparingly, and move to what's next?

TIP #91

Shift From Why to What's Next?

Do you spend too much time in the land of *whys*? Although it is a land to visit now and again, you don't want to spend your life there.

Whys have their place in gaining insight and finding reasons for how you have developed, but often too much focus on *whys* makes you a victim of the past and keeps you a prisoner.

One thing about the past–it never changes!

How about freeing yourself from the chains of the past by focusing on what's next? How about making an action plan and change your questions into goals?

Make a list of up to four *why* questions in your life that keep you stuck:

1.

2.

3.

4.

Now answer each why question with what's next? For example, "*Why am I so sensitive?*" can be transformed to: "*I tend to be shy when speaking in groups. To help me with this tendency, I will write down my negative thoughts that make me anxious and work on replacing them with healthier ones.*"

Or instead of wondering why your coworker is so rude, make it into a goal, such as: "When he acts rudely, I will tell him I will not continue our discussion until he addresses me more respectfully."

For each of your answers above, transform them into an action plan of "*what's next?*"

1.

2.

3.

4.

So next time, instead of getting stuck in the *whys*, why not wise up and move on to *what's next?*

Remember, it is not *wise* to ask too many *whys*!

TIP #92

Why Not?

Why questions do have their place, but not if they keep you stuck reworking the past. Perhaps the most forward-looking why question you could ask yourself is *why not?* Too many times we stop ourselves from trying new things and taking risks in making changes in our lives because the unknown paralyzes us. When this happens, how about asking yourself *why not?*

When you are fearful of speaking up, ask yourself, *why not?*

_____

If you hesitate to take a chance to try something new that has no certainties, ask yourself, *why not?*

_____

If you are not happy with the way your life is going and you want to make major changes, ask yourself, *why not?*

_____

Afraid to pursue your dreams in case they flop? Ask yourself, *why not?*

_____

You might find that fear, anxiety, insecurity, and uncertainty get in the way of pursuing your dreams. Do you really want to define yourself by your doubts and disappointments, or would you like to be defined by your dreams and determination?

What's stopping you? Pursue your dreams—you have one shot at life! Why not?

7

Improving Communication, *Improving Relationships*

TIPS 93–105

TIP #93
Improving Communication, Improving Relationships

THEORY: The importance of assertive communication skills cannot be over-emphasized. Communication skills determine the quality of our relationships, yet many people are lacking in even the most basic knowledge of the guidelines for good communication. This results in miscommunication, and the fallout results in unhealthy relationships. Interpersonal Effectiveness is a cornerstone of the DBT group model, and was introduced in TIPS 64-65. This chapter provides additional materials since interpersonal communication and interpersonal relationships is the focus of just about any therapeutic orientation. As most therapists would agree, relationship issues are often a primary or secondary problem that brings most of our clients to therapy, so almost any therapist can benefit from some additional materials for relationship skill building.

The handouts and worksheets in this section provide further differentiation between the three major types of communication, and they give plenty of opportunity to recognize and practice assertive skills.

It has been estimated that approximately 85 percent of the reasons why people fail at their jobs is not due to a lack of technical ability, but due to problems in communication. So your client's personal and professional success depends on it!

Since people are sorely lacking in the *how-tos* of communication, this section offers ideas and practice opportunities so that people can build their interpersonal skills.

IMPLEMENTATION: Understanding the three types of communication and being able to distinguish between them is particularly useful and handouts, such as TIP 94, have provided countless clients insight into their own communication styles.

I use a basic sheet such as this one in my very first session with couples, to lay a foundation of healthy vs. unhealthy communication. For example, even when someone has come into the office angry and aggressive toward their spouse, when I show them this sheet and explain the three types of communication, they willingly identify themselves as aggressive. It never fails to amaze me that the most aggressive, defensive spouses will correctly identify themselves as aggressive when seeing it on paper, despite the fact that before presentation of the handout, they deny having major communication problems. *Thus, their insight does not come from me, it comes from them!*

We can then refer to their aggressive behavior without them getting defensive because they described themselves that way–it was not me or their spouse! This TIP not only highlights the problem and educates, but serves as a blueprint they can refer to over and over again for guidelines to good communication and great alternatives. Many of the worksheets in this section will help your clients practice skills at home, to be processed in the session.

The sheets also provide a great springboard for role-playing both in individual and group sessions.

PROCESSING: With the help of these practical handouts, clients can identify their patterns and identify their style of communication. Often these patterns are learned early on and often are a product of socialization (e.g., women are more rewarded in some societies for being non-assertive, men for being more aggressive). Make it a point to share with your clients that communication is not only good for relationships, it is good for them! People who express themselves freely and stand up for what they believe in are generally less anxious, more confident, happier people than their more *aggressive* or *non-assertive* counterparts.

TIP #94
THE THREE BASIC TYPES OF COMMUNICATION

All communication can fit into these three types of communication styles. **Assertive is the healthiest and most ideal.** Under stress and in times of conflict, people who are normally assertive in most situations sometimes resort to either non-assertive or aggressive communication. Often our patterns of communication differ with our different relationships. *In fact, the closer people are to us, the more we tend to be aggressive under stress!* It seems that the more there is at stake, the more we want them to change!

The Three Types of Communication

	NON-ASSERTIVE	AGGRESSIVE	ASSERTIVE
Message	"You're okay, I'm not." "You're better than me"	"I'm okay, you're not." "I'm better than you."	"I'm okay–you're okay." "We are both worthy"
Description	Keeps thoughts and feelings in Low self-confidence Allows others to walk on them Fear of making waves or conflict–Inhibited Emotionally dishonest Judges self Indirect, beats around the bush	"You" Statements Over-confident Infringes on the rights of others View others as "starting it" Let's it out–little filtering Honest without tact Judges others Too direct	"I" Statements Confident Respects your rights and others Compromising w/o arguing Speaks openly but tactful Honest but tactful Non-judgmental Direct with tact
Attitude	Self-critical Quietly resentful Intimidated Too pre-occupied to really listen	Criticizes others Resentful–and shows it Condescending Dismissive, not listening	Accepting Disappointed but not vengeful Respectful Can "listen"–not just "hear"
Goal	Wants to be liked Needy for approval Wants to change to please others Self-protective	Invalidating Needs to be right above all Wants to change others Vengeful, "gets back"	Validating to self and others Strives for a balance Only changes themselves Sets healthy boundaries
Feelings	Anxious, fearful, guilty Depression common Feels like a "victim" Self-blaming	Feeling Superior Self-Righteous Suspicious Blames everyone else	Even-tempered w/ healthy regret Feels good Feels like a "victor" Takes responsibility
Secondary Gain	Avoids risk, seeks safety Changes self to please others Doesn't want to be wrong	Micromanages situation Changes others to please self Wants to be right	Manages own reactions Changes self only Tries their best
Note:	Non-assertion often results in aggression	Might be passive aggressive	Might not get what they want

TIP #95

How Do YOU Communicate?

What is your communication style? Considering the three types of communication, choose what fits you best.

People do not usually act one way only—their behavior changes according to their relationship, their stress level, and the situation that triggers their reactions.

How do you act in general when not under excess stress?

_____

How do you generally act in times of stress with your **family members**? Respond where it applies.

Parents_____

Spouse_____

Children_____

Siblings_____

Relatives_____

How do you generally act in times of stress with **friends and community**? Respond where it applies.

Friends_____

Boyfriend/girlfriend_____

Neighbors_____

Members of secular and non-secular groups which I belong_____

How do you generally act in times of stress at **work or school**? Respond where it applies.

Coworkers_____

Supervisors_____

Employees_____

Customers_____

Clients_____

Students_____

Teachers_____

What areas do I need to work on to develop my assertive skills?

_____

TIP #96

What's Your Communication Motto?

The images of the bull, eagle and doormat can help you remember the three types of communication. Are you more like a bull (aggressive), a doormat (non-assertive) or an eagle (assertive)? *In general, what is your communication motto?*

Bull

"I have more power than you!"

"I can prove it!"

"Might makes right."

"I won't give up trying to change others who need my advice!"

"I know what's best!"

Eagle

"I strive to improve, not prove"

"I will only teach if the student is willing."

"I will try to change what I can and accept the rest"

"I only know what is best for me, and that can change as I grow!"

Doormat

"I'm going to play it safe!"

"I need people to like me so I don't want to make them mad!"

"I HATE conflict and will avoid it above all!"

"It would be terrible if they are mad at me or don't like me!"

"I have to protect myself above all, even if it means denying my rights."

How would you like to improve your communication?

_____

What will be your new motto?

_____

How can you keep "on track?"

_____

TIP #97

My Assertive Bill of Rights

Want to increase your chances of success? **Tell someone about it!** Research has shown that those who tell someone are most likely to succeed. Who can you enlist help from for feedback and support?

I have a right to be wrong!

I have a right to express my thoughts and feelings.

I have a right to regard my needs as just as important as anyone else's.

I have a right to be happy, regardless of how many mistakes I made in the past.

I have a right to be treated respectfully.

I have a right for my needs to be as important as others.

I have a right to set limits.

I have a right to pursue happiness, even if it might not be approved of by others.

I have a right to decide what is best for me.

I have a right not to live up to other people's expectations of me.

I have a right to make mistakes.

I have a right to not be perfect.

I have a right to expect to be treated with respect.

I have a right to feel angry, sad, disappointed.

I have a right to heal.

I have a right to forgive myself and others.

I have a right to love myself regardless of my imperfections.

I have a right to stand up for what I believe in.

I have a right to say "no," even if others are disappointed.

I have a right to change my mind.

I have a right not to be responsible for other people's happiness—only my own.

What other personalized rights can you add to the list?

I have a right to _____

I have a right to _____

I have a right to _____

I have a right to _____

TIP #98

My Assertive Responsibilities

Along with our rights, we have corresponding responsibilities. Below are some examples of rights and the corresponding responsibilities.

I have a **right** to be wrong!

I have a **responsibility** to try my best, without expecting perfection!

I have a **right** to express my thoughts and feelings.

I have a **responsibility** to express myself tactfully and assertively in a way that harm is not intended.

I have a **right** to regard my needs as just as important as anyone else's needs.

I have a **responsibility** to express my needs while being sensitive to those of others.

I have a **right** to be happy, regardless of how many mistakes I made in the past.

I have a **responsibility** to make amends if my actions were hurtful: to apologize, take responsibility and try better in the future to learn from the feedback of mistakes that were made. Using mistakes as feedback will help me make better choices now.

Now it's your turn. In the space below, write down other rights and corresponding responsibilities that relate to you.

Right: _____

Responsibility: _____

Right: _____

Responsibility: _____

Right: _____

Responsibility: _____

Right: _____

Responsibility: _____

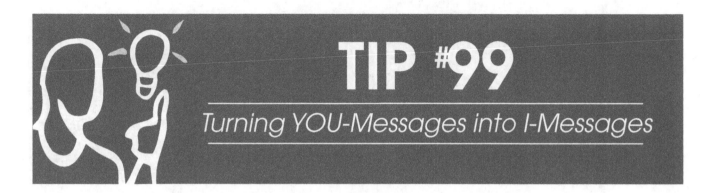

TIP #99

Turning YOU-Messages into I-Messages

Turn aggressive YOU-statements into I-statements. After the first two examples, try to fill in the rest.

YOU-Statement: "You should have done this by now–you never listen!"

I-Statement: "I am frustrated that when I tell you often about doing this, it does not get done and you seem to be ignoring me. Any thoughts on this?"

YOU-Statement: "You are so rude! You can't talk to me that way!"

I-Statement: "I am not comfortable when you put me down and criticize the way I act. I find it disrespectful."

NOW IT'S YOUR TURN!

YOU-Statement: "Stop blaming me for things that are not my fault!"

I-Statement:

_____

YOU- Statement: "That was not what happened! I can't believe you said that!"

I-Statement:

_____

YOU- Statement: "That will never work!"

I-Statement:

_____

YOU- Statement: "I'm tired of you complaining all the time–you are so ungrateful!"

I-Statement:

_____

YOU- Statement: "When are you going to start being respectful?"

I-Statement:

_____

Can you think of your own?

_____

_____

TIP #100

My Reflections of My Rights and My Responsibilities

What are at least three rights I will work on accepting actively in my daily life?

1. _____

2. _____

3. _____

Specifically, how will I do this?

1. _____

2. _____

3. _____

What are my corresponding responsibilities?

1. _____

2. _____

3. _____

How would my life be different if I really accepted these rights?

_____

What have been the costs in my life for not fully accepting these rights?

_____

How can I support myself and seek support from others to keep working on accepting my rights?

_____

TIP #101

Assertive, Non-Assertive, Aggressive–Can You Tell Them Apart?

This checklist offers examples that characterize the three types of communication. Next to each item, write the initials of which behavior it describes and then check your answers with the key at the bottom.

A - Assertive: Respectful and tactful

AG - Aggressive: Controlling and tactless

NA - Non-Assertive: Anxious, self-denying, avoiding

_____ 1. Giving the cold shoulder.

_____ 2. Beating around the bush, being indirect.

_____ 3. You decide not to assert yourself when your friend's behavior bothers you, not out of fear, but because you see this person very little and decide you do not want to say anything

_____ 4. You don't say anything about something that bothers you, because you know it might set the person off.

_____ 5. You say, "I feel like you are hurting my feelings all the time and you don't even know it!"

_____ 6. You take offense when your coworker jokes about things that are bothering you, and you say, "Why don't you take me seriously?"

_____ 7. Too nervous to make a mistake, you remain silent in a meeting.

_____ 8. Someone says to you, "You've been anxious about this ever since I met you, and you still are!"

_____ 9. Your parent tells you that you are too sensitive.

_____ 10. When your family member tells you that you are too sensitive, you say, "That isn't right to label me–that's aggressive!"

_____ 11. It is hard for your spouse to forgive you for something that you have already apologized for many times, and you ask, "When are you going to move on from the past and get over it?"

_____ 12. You are frustrated with your child's rudeness and say, "You can't talk to me that way!"

_____ 13. Your friend is late again and you say, "Why are you so late again?"

_____ 14. Your boss criticizes you and you say, "I do not mind you correcting me, but I feel disrespected and am asking you to be less personal about my shortcomings."

_____ 15. "I felt very uncomfortable when you said that to me."

ANSWER KEY: 1.AG, 2.NA, 3.A, 4.NA, 5.AG, 6.AG, 7.NA, 8.AG, 9.AG, 10.AG, 11.AG, 12.AG, 13.AG, 14.A, 15.A

TIP #102

Rate Your Communication Style

This self-test will help you reflect on your own communication style. There is another scale following for a close friend or family member to fill out about you. Do not show one another the answers until you finish–how do they compare? This can be extremely enlightening for spouses to fill out this sheet and then also rate one another and compare answers. This will likely be quite an eye opener, because the way you see yourself is not always the way others see you!

Agree	Somewhat Agree	Uncertain	Somewhat Disagree	Disagree
1	2	3	4	5

_____ I do not hold grudges.

_____ I am accepting of others and their differences from me.

_____ I speak my mind with tact.

_____ I am confident in how I talk to others.

_____ I am able to apologize when I am wrong.

_____ I stand up for myself if I feel disrespected.

_____ I like who I am and I show it in the way I carry myself.

_____ I am respectful in my communication with others, including children.

_____ I am more of a stress manager than a stress carrier (I handle my stress well).

_____ I show empathy and caring freely.

Add up the items. The total score is _____

In all the above items, the lower you score, the more you have an assertive communication style.

10-15: You are quite assertive and confident!

16-23: You are generally assertive and confident.

24-30: You are having some trouble with staying assertive

31-40: You communication needs work–you have trouble keeping assertive

41 and above: You are in danger of jeopardizing your relationships! Needs improvement NOW!

TIP #103

Rate How You Think They Communicate!

Before rating one another, make sure each of you fill out your own self-rating questionnaire in TIP 102. This will make for a very interesting discussion about your communication styles!

Agree	Somewhat Agree	Uncertain	Somewhat Disagree	Disagree
1	2	3	4	5

_____ He/she does not hold grudges.

_____ He/she is accepting of others and their differences.

_____ He/she speaks his/her mind with tact.

_____ He/she is confident in how he/she talks to others.

_____ He/she is able to apologize when he/she is wrong.

_____ He/she stands up for herself/himself if he/she feels disrespected.

_____ He/she carries himself/herself with self-esteem and confidence.

_____ He/she is respectful in communicating with others, including children.

_____ He/she is more of a stress manager (who handles stress well) than a stress carrier!

_____ He/she shows empathy and caring freely.

Add up the items. The total score is _____

In all the above items, the lower the score, the more you consider their communication assertive.

10-15: You see him/her as quite assertive and confident!

16-23: You see him/her as generally assertive and confident.

24-30: You see him/her as having some trouble with staying assertive.

31-40: He/she appears to need work on communicating assertively.

41 and above: Your relationship is likely problematic! Needs attention NOW!

TIP #104

Rhetorical Questions: Put-Downs in Disguise!

"Did you really just say that?"
"Am I the only one that does work around here?"
"Didn't I already tell you that?"

We are all familiar with rhetorical questions, but few people really know how aggressive they are! Rhetorical questions are really aggressive statements disguised as questions. They are not meant to be answered! The purpose is not to validate and empathize but to "prove a point" and to "put down." For example, if a parent says to a child, "How many times did I tell you to put your shoes away?" The mom or dad is not really expecting an answer, like 159 times. Who's really counting?

Because rhetorical questions are so common in everyday life, often insults and sarcasm go under the radar due to their clever disguise as questions! They might be unsettling for the recipient, but most people don't realize they were spoken down to so aggressively.

The accompanying table gives you examples of rhetorical questions and gives you a chance to fill in some of your own as well. This will help you identify this type of disguised aggression and learn how to respond.

Put a check mark next to each rhetorical question that either you say or that you hear others say. Then write an assertive alternative for each, taking away the judgmental quality.

Rhetorical Question	Assertive Alternative (descriptive, not judgmental)
What's wrong with you?	*I am frustrated when you yell at me.*
Don't you listen?	
Are you going to wear THAT?	
Why can't you just stop doing that?	
How many times do I need to remind you?	

Write your own rhetorical question and then rephrase an assertive alternative.

Rhetorical Question: _____

_____

Assertive Alternative: _____

_____

TIP #105

Checklist for Being Assertive

Here are some tips to keep you on the assertive track! Use this as a guideline when you practice your assertive skills! Great for practicing!

✓ **Use "I" Statements.** You still can use the word "you," just like I did in this sentence! "You" is not a bad word–although you-statements should be avoided! The difference? A you-statement is judgmental and telling someone what they should do. You have strings attached to your communication. *Note:* Just because you start with an "I" does not mean you are home free! For example, "I think you stink" is aggressive no matter how you look at it!

✓ **Clarify the major points you want to say.** Be specific and descriptive to ask someone for a change in their behavior, stick to the facts and clarify a few points, rehearse if there is time.

✓ **Ask yourself: "Is my goal assertive?"** Keep your goal in mind. Many times people think their goal is assertive, but it is actually aggressive even if it is well-meaning. Why? Because just trying to change someone's mind, trying to get them to see your point of view and to be understood are all things you have no control over. You can't change their perceptions and you can't reach in and change their neurons! You can talk until you are blue in the face, and someone might still not "get it." An assertive goal is merely to express yourself and is not contingent on the other person "getting it!"

✓ **Make sure your self-talk is assertive!** It will be hard to pull off being assertive if you are thinking in aggressive ways. If you have too many *shoulds* on someone else, you will likely have an aggressive goal. If your self-talk is assertive, you will more likely assert yourself!

✓ **Don't get sidetracked!** I often say to my clients, *"Don't be led around like a pony."* We live in a world where all sorts of things can come at you. Stay focused on what you want to express, even if you have to keep repeating yourself like a broken record. That's called the *broken record technique.*

✓ **Don't over-apologize!** Although it is good to apologize if you did something you regret, over-apologizing becomes about you needing that other person to like you. Don't give up so much power!

✓ **Empathize and validate, while still standing your ground.** Just because you care about what they feel or think, does not mean you have to cave in if that would be disregarding your own rights.

✓ **Fit your non-verbals to match your verbal message.** If you have poor eye contact, look down, fidget or have your voice waiver, you will not come across assertively even if you say the right words. Assertiveness takes practice both verbally and non-verbally. How about practicing in front of a mirror?

WHEN IT COMES TO
RELATIONSHIPS,
BUILD BRIDGES
NOT WALLS

Social Media for Mental Health and Wellness

TIPS 106–116

TIP #106

Social Media Tips for Your Mental Health Message, Products and Practice

THEORY: There is a new frontier for mental health professionals, and it is known as *Social Media*. For those like me who were trained before the internet age (I certainly was when I got my M.S. in Clinical Psychology in 1977). At that time, computers were huge mainframes the size of a room! The ways of promoting your mental health message, your practice, your products and your books were quite limited–mostly through print media. With the advances in technology and cyberspace, a whole new world is open to promote you and your message! And with increasingly "user-friendly" websites and services, you can actually be fairly proficient, pretty quickly, especially if you enlist some technology help!

The power of social media for mental health practitioners is dauntingly enormous. We have amazing potential to do our part to help heal the world through our mental health message and products. We can reach far and wide.

There is certainly no "one size fits all." However, there are some well-established paths that seem to yield the most rewards for increasing visibility that I have found so far on my own journey through social media cyberspace. Although social media can be time consuming, especially in the trial and error phase as you see what fits, getting some of the following practical tips and information for your social media toolbox will help you be more direct and streamlined in your approach. If you are establishing yourself as a mental health expert, whether it is in your clinic, your community, or even at the national level and beyond, you likely don't want to spend a whole lot of time figuring out also how to be a social media expert! After all, we signed up to be clinicians, not *techies*.

This section is designed to give you a very quick overview of various social media sites that are relevant to the mental health field, to give you an advantage in mental health cyberspace!

IMPLEMENTATION: What I expected when I began my own social media journey ended up quite differently. After *The Swiss Cheese Theory of Life* was published, I spent a great deal of time trying to figure out how social media could increase book sales.

Very quickly, however, my goals shifted from book sales to promoting my passion for wellness through a couple channels that appealed to my interests and creative skills: guest blogging and making original inspirational posts. What started out as an attempt to gain exposure for my books became not at all about the books, but about spreading the message of positivity in the world, and receiving lots of positivity back in different ways. It has helped me as a clinician, a speaker, a workplace wellness trainer, and as a writer.

I evolved a social media presence that now gains new Facebook fans each week, and have enjoyed being part of a worldwide community of people who are passionate about wellness, personal development and positivity.

PROCESSING: To help me compile this section, I have asked for comments, testimonials and tips through Facebook, LinkedIn and Twitter from other professionals and self-help enthusiasts from around the world. Their comments are sprinkled all around this section. The wonderful thing about social media is that you get instant access to many people you would normally never get to know, and you can learn from them through their sites, blogs, and posts.

Earlier this year, I only used Facebook occasionally, in order to keep in touch with family members and friends. As I started getting interested in posting inspirational quotes, I have met many people who share the same passion, and have been inspired by their work. I learn from their creativity and from social media fans and followers who genuinely appreciate learning and sharing in this very global community.

The testimonials in this section reveal the attraction of Facebook and other social media that can promote mental health messages all over the world. If we, as therapists, can offer mental health insights of inspiration and positivity, just think how much more healing there can be in the world!

There are direct and indirect gains from so much exposure, and this section is just a basic introduction to cyberspace potential. For those who are more interested in promoting a local counseling practice, social media is also quite helpful in attracting new clients and establishing your visibility in your community. So whether the community you want to reach is a local community or a global community, social media offers something for everyone!

This is certainly not meant to be a complete *how-to* guide to social media. This is an overview where I offer my own tips and tools that I have found useful in the wellness/mental health space, and mention some great sites and resources I have discovered on my journey in cyberspace. It is an ever growing field, and here are the basics to get you either started or jumpstart you to the *next level*.

In this chapter, I picked only social media outlets that are very popular and have worked well for me in expanding my platform for speaking, selling books, and promoting mental health. Even if promoting a book or your services is the initial reason to plunge into social media on a professional level, if you are like me, you will soon find that this worldwide community offers you a wellness boost that you could never have imagined!

In this section, I have included many comments and testimonials of people who have both positive inspirational and wellness sites to show you the power of social media and the message. I have also highlighted a few sites, out of the many that are available, that are wonderful examples of the power of positivity and emotional wellness.

* All of the quotes with attributions have the originator's permission.

TIP #107

Quick Tips for a Successful Mental Health Website

THEORY: With the increasing use of the internet in everyday life, mental health practitioners who want to promote their practice will likely find it very helpful to have their own website. For those without websites, it might seem too time-consuming and daunting to even think of establishing one. However, if you have a limited scope of having an on-line presence to attract new clients, it does not have to be a costly or exhaustive endeavor. Websites are increasingly user-friendly and if you want, your site can be just a couple pages and can be quite limited in scope. For those who want to have a more extensive website on which to promote a book or other products, including speaking, it obviously will take more time to develop and will cost more to be developed. Wordpress has also some *do-it-yourself* programs to walk you through doing you own site with minimal knowledge.

Building your social media platform is like building a house: You have an idea of the house (your website) that you want to build and how it will look (your website design), and it takes an architect (web designer) to put it on paper. You could have your house designed from scratch, which is costly, or you could use a general plan that is readily available and modify it for you own needs (that is what a Wordpress template does). Once you have a house designed, you need to find a location for it to be built, so you need an address (your domain name). You also need to have it maintained, repaired and kept up-to-date (your website host).

IMPLEMENTATION: Whether you are promoting your local private practice, or trying to reach an audience much wider to promote your book, services, products, or speaking events, the web has something for everyone. Potential clients often look on the web to screen potential therapists and having a web presence can take some of the guesswork out of going to talk to someone that they know nothing about, and this way they feel like they are not going to a *complete stranger.*

Having a blog that you update even occasionally with a mental health message not only attracts new clients but keeps your current clients engaged. Even if you do not have the time or desire to update even short blogs, having a website where you have your background, picture, interests, specialties, etc. can be quite helpful in maintaining your visibility in your community.

There are certainly other ways to have a web presence besides a website. Having a Facebook business page is free, and this is different than your personal friend and family page which will be explained in TIP 110. *Psychology Today* provides a database which potential clients can search by Zip Code, specialties and other information, and you can be listed for a fee.

If you do not have a website already, and are contemplating having one, this is a great time to have one developed. With the advent of Wordpress-type web sites, having a site created by a web developer can be very affordable and designed in a way that you can learn to easily update with some simple instructions. Years back, my first websites were written in complex computer language, and without a programming background, were impossible for me to make even minor changes, and it was costly to have my web developers make changes for me. Now I have everything converted over to Wordpress sites, which have a plain English interface, and I can maintain them myself quite easily once I have them designed, with occasional help for more complex tasks.

Having a website developed by a designer is cheaper and easier than ever before using templates. The template that I had my web designer use is Wordpress Studio Genesis. For less than a hundred dollars, you can purchase a template from the many available. This significantly reduces the cost of a web designer's time, compared to having a custom-made web site.

To find a developer, I have posted both on guru.com which has been a fabulous resource to find people to help with logos, web design, etc. (you get to see their ratings and recommendations) and also craigslist.com. In the past, my website development had been more costly due to the older technology available for website development. After a couple phone tutorials with my web developer, I learned how to make changes very easily if I want to update my site.

As for hosting, there are many hosting sites vying for your business. I personally have been happy with one of the biggest and more popular hosting sites, Go Daddy (godaddy.com). From hosting sites, you can buy domains for other site ideas you might have in the future.

PROCESSING: The following TIPS in this section are by no means everything you need to know about having a mental health website, but they do provide some of the basic framework to make it easier for you to build your virtual cyberhouse!

TIP #108

Guest Blogging for Wellness

THEORY: You can write the most amazing blog, but if you have little traffic to your site, very few people can see it. Unless you are already famous in your own right, you likely will be starting out with relatively few subscribers and viewers to your blog. No one will hear you say *I'm here* when you click *post* and your new blog post appears for the world to see on your site. It's like having a wonderful dance performance and having only a few people scattered around the audience. For the same effort you put in, wouldn't you rather have a packed house for your performance? That is the beauty of guest posts! The best way to get more visibility for you and your site, as well as your books, products and your speaking, is to guest blog on other sites that are in the personal development/mental health and wellness field.

IMPLEMENTATION: Successful blog posts are relatively short pieces that are often broken up with small bites of information, bullet points, bold headings, etc. People do not read long narrative blogs. They are looking for quick tips, and numbered lists with a short intro and conclusion seems to fit the bill!

For example, in TIP 109 I have included my guest post from a popular site, Life Hack, titled *The Top 10 Habits of Grateful People...Even in Tough Times.*

I received a lot of exposure from that one post with thousands of social media mentions through tweets, Stumble Upon recommendations, Facebook and LinkedIn re-postings. In turn, I got many new subscribers to my newsletter and more traffic driven to my site.

When looking for potential guest post sites, widening your scope to look for any sites that have a lifestyle, motivation, or wellness component in it might reach a larger audience than those only in the mental health realm. Most people have more than just a passing interest in happiness, well-being and leading a more fulfilling life, so popular sites that encompass these areas, such as Life Hack type sites can give you thousands of viewers for your post, which in turn, will drive traffic to your social media sites with your bio and links to your own sites.

Not only will these viewers help drive traffic back to your site, they might also tweet, post to Facebook and LinkedIn, submit your blog to Google + (which is Google's alternative to Facebook), Pinterest, and other social media sites, so you can build a following on various sites by submitting one blog post.

How do you know which are well trafficked sites? Alexa (alexa.com) is an amazing web tool that can offer you valuable information about how popular any site is. The smaller the number, the better. If a score to a web site is in the millions, that is a very low trafficked site. If the site is in double digit thousands, then it is fairly well travelled, and if it is in the thousands (in the US in particular), then you have a great guest blog site potential.

You then need to check out their policies to see if they accept guest posts and their requirements for posting. I have found that what worked the best for me is that I started out making a few guest posts–snappy short posts that had lists and bullets and sent them off to the websites that I googled in the area of personal development with good Alexa rankings and kept resubmitting to other sites (with less traffic) if I was either ignored or rejected, and eventually my posts were accepted. After all if you spend some time making a post, you want to make sure people see it!

Another way to find popular guest blog opportunities is comment on posts in your niche. Commenting on relevant sites will automatically link back to your own site if you sign up for free services like Disqus and Comment Luv.

When you do a guest post, part of the expectation is that you answer each and every comment that people write in response to your post. That gives you and your message even more exposure and a wider reach!

PROCESSING: Guest blogging on well trafficked sites will help establish your platform as an expert and drive traffic to your social media sites. It has also been very rewarding to spread inspirational messages for positive living and emotional wellness!

TIP 109 is one of my more popular sample guest posts from a great life skills site, lifehack.org.

TIP #109

The Top 10 Habits of Grateful People... Even in Tough Times

"Gratitude is the fairest blossom which springs from the soul."

— *Henry Ward Beecher (1813-1887)*

It is no secret that gratefulness is correlated with life satisfaction and happiness. Countless research findings, particularly in the rapidly emerging field of Positive Psychology, have shown that gratefulness and life satisfaction go hand in hand. Those who tend to be more grateful rather than bitter are generally more positive, more satisfied with their lives, and will be able to see the silver lining even on cloudy days.

Despite this intuitive understanding of the importance of gratefulness, all too often when life throws us curve balls, this grateful mindset all but disappears. It certainly is easier to be grateful when you are on a winning team and things go in your favor. However, the true test of resiliency and gratefulness is when life does not go your way. If you find yourself losing more than you are winning, and can't seem to get over past regrets, disappointments and life's injustices, gratefulness is overturned by a sense of injustice. Experiencing loss, frustration and even trauma, especially if we feel blindsided, certainly can make it difficult not to indulge in negative feelings. After all, we might wonder, when things go wrong what really do we have to be grateful about?

No matter what happens to us, if we "dig deep" we often can find that there is really plenty to be thankful for in our lives. The following are the top 10 habits of people who remain steadfast in their ability to be grateful, and can temper the blows life gives them with an unwavering *attitude of gratitude* mindset:

1. Grateful people don't expect that life is going to give them everything they deserve. They realize that good things do not always happen to good people, and they have given up the notion that life "owes them" anything more than it can offer. Cancer, afflictions, and even the death of innocent people are unfortunately part of life. Tsunamis and natural disasters can wipe out a community of unsuspecting people, and the unfairness of life is regrettable and tragic for sure. The question is not if life is unfair, but can we move on in spite of it.

2. They do not have preconditions to their happiness. They do not think "If this happens" only then "I will be happy." They understand happiness is not coming from the outside, but from within. They focus more on their adjustment to what happens rather than try to change what cannot be changed. They do not attempt to micromanage people and things in their lives that are not really in their control.

3. People who are grateful have realized that you cannot have the rainbow without the rain. Furthermore, they know that you don't have honey without the bee, and you can't have the rose without the thorns. They see rainy days as a normal part of life rather than an aberration, and learn from the rain rather than just wait for it to go away. They admire the beauty of the rose even though it has its thorny side, and savor the sweet taste of honey even though the bee can sting. Realizing you cannot have one without the other, they are grateful for both.

4. Grateful people have hope. No matter what happens, hope is not lost. They realize the future is uncertain, and while they plan for it, they do not try to micromanage outcomes that are beyond their sphere of influence. They

take comfort in the fact that once the sun sets, it rises the next day. They have faith that there is more to life. They hack life rather than feel hacked by life.

5. Those who are steeped in bitterness and grudges have no space in their heart to be grateful. Forgiving your spouse for not being as understanding as you would have been, forgiving your children for making choices that would not have been your own, and giving up the grudge of a slight or injustice from a friend, are all parts of the gratitude equation. Forgive others for not acting or being like you had hoped. Maybe you need to set limits on your interaction with them, or distance yourself altogether as in the case of abuse, but carrying the torch of bitterness is going to hurt you more than them. As Buddha said, "Holding onto anger is like grasping a hot coal with the intent of throwing it at someone else; you are the one who gets burned."

6. People who are grateful know that a grateful attitude takes work. Gratefulness does not always come naturally, especially in the most challenging times. In such times, grateful people work on keeping a good perspective. They might read affirmations, seek support from others, and get help for their sadness or anxiety. Some will seek counseling and do not shy away from the effort it takes.

7. Grateful people have healthy thinking habits. They go by the motto, "Think Straight–Feel Great!" They can separate their perceptions from the facts and separate rational from victim-like irrational ways of thinking. For example, they will replace victim self-talk such as "They make me so mad" to victor self-talk such as "I was mad when they did that." All-or-nothing irrational thinking such as "It's awful" and "I can't stand it" is reserved for the most life threatening circumstance, rather than everyday petty annoyances and slights.

8. Grateful people are flexible in their thinking. People who think flexibly are at an advantage in life, as flexibility is the key to growth and wisdom. They don't cling stubbornly with ways of thinking that do not work, and do not need to see a shift in attitude as meaning a personal defeat and referendum of how wrong they used to be. They realize they can choose their perceptions and have a right to change their minds. With this mentality, the doors that close yield to others that now become open.

9. People who love to learn tend to be grateful. Each setback or unforeseen life event offers us lessons, and grateful people focus more on the lessons they can get out of each situation rather than the disappointments. After all, life is a great teacher and teaches us things that no one ever could. Even mistakes and failures are seen as learning opportunities.

10. Grateful people define their self-worth by their determination and their dreams, not their regrets and disappointments. A grateful mindset has no room for excessive self-recrimination and low self-esteem. People who are stuck in past regrets and see themselves as losers in life or having failed badly in even certain areas of their lives will not be able to be truly grateful. Positive self-esteem sets the foundation for gratefulness. So if you are down on yourself, this is a time to get a mental health tune up!

How about starting a Gratefulness campaign in your own life? Start now by writing down at least 10 things you are thankful for. How about sharing some of them by commenting below?

(By the way…thanks for reading. I am very grateful!)

TIP #110

Facebook Wellness

Facebook has amazing potential for disseminating your mental health message, connecting with a local as well as a worldwide audience, AND for gaining support and inspiration from other mental health and personal development sites. It is often much more dynamic than a web site. People might visit several times a day if you update your own or shared inspirational posts from other pages, and commenting on and sharing posts from other pages is very easy with the share button.

Those interested in positive psychology and cognitive therapy would likely enjoy visiting Facebook's inspirational and mental health sites. The ones that I am interested in are ones that focus on emotional wellness and positive living!

With an audience of millions, there are of course many ways to use Facebook, and this TIP will by no means do more than scratch the surface of its vast potential. Even if you decide not to have your own Facebook business page, you might enjoy seeing what other people in the mental health and wellness space are doing to promote positive wellness around the world.

IMPLEMENTATION: For those who have a website, Facebook can do wonders to direct people to it, and for those without a website, you still can have a web presence with a Facebook page for your counseling practice.

Here are some tips that you need to know if you have your own business page on Facebook:

With regards to Facebook, there is some controversy about whether therapists should have a Facebook page that clients can "friend." In a guest blog post on the American Counseling Association website, I addressed this issue in response to another guest post questioning the merits or even ethics of having a Facebook page to which clients can have access. With limited knowledge of Facebook, I can see why that would be seen as crossing the line of personal and professional boundaries, i.e. to "friend" clients on Facebook. However, with a more in-depth understanding of how Facebook works, the lines do not have to be blurred at all.

I do agree that to have your clients be so privy to your personal life can wreak havoc with transference and blurs boundaries. I really cannot see any good use for Facebook when therapists use their personal page. However, the benefits of having a separate Facebook business page to promote mental health and wellness are invaluable. I have a completely separate professional "friend" page where anyone is welcome (Judith Belmont is my personal page and Judy Belmont is my professional one), and I have attached my professional friend page to my business page (you cannot have a business page without linking it to a personal page). Thus, your friends on this business page are only people who friend you through your page and they have has no access to personal information. In any of my guest blogs or promotional material, I only will publish to my business friend page, never my personal one.

The goal of a business page, called a Fan Page, is to get "likes" (there is a "like" button on a Fan Page that someone can press to get your updates). People who like you usually get your updated posts in their Facebook feeds (depending on the settings chosen).

After having a Facebook business page set up, mostly to promote my books, I was all set up and nowhere to go!

I saw on LinkedIn that people were asking others to reciprocate Facebook likes to boost their fan following, but it was a lot of work for very little success. I started checking out other sites in the mental health and wellness space and was struck by the wealth of beautiful inspirational posts which consisted of original or famous quotes and beautiful pictures. I enjoyed looking at them and found them to be very uplifting, and started trying to create them myself. I used some of my own pictures and some I bought from inexpensive royalty free services as backdrops and found it to be a great forum to put forth my own inspirational thoughts and quotes, and quickly increased my fan base by trading shares with other sites like mine.

So from the Philippines, to the UK, to India and Nepal, I have joined a community of lovely souls who have, as their mission, to inspire and promote positivity. My clients have loved keeping track of my posts and my shares from other sites.

What started for me as a forum to promote my books became a general mission to promote the message of mental health and wellness. I have been amazed at the positive response from people all around the world to messages of self-empowerment, forgiveness, gratitude, healthy parenting, positive thinking and other cornerstones of mental wellness.

I have found that my own personal mental wellness has risen a few notches by exploring and sharing other mental health sites. I believe this has made me a better clinician, as well as a better author and speaker. For counselors who want to widen their repertoire of services and resources they offer, social media is invaluable.

PROCESSING: How about having your client make up their own inspirational quotes and even posts, after showing them some from the web or your own self-created ones? Use it as my clients sometimes do as backgrounds on phones and computers.

The following are a sample of the many testimonials that I have received to show you the power of inspirational posts and promoting positivity on Facebook. These responses represent the type of responses I have seen on many other websites as well, so they are posted here to show merely the power of using social media to promote mental health around the globe. All are printed with permission.

"It's been one week since I found this site. And I've already become more positive in dealing with each day. Thank you for your pics and quotes that you share from other sites. It's very inspiring."

Mymoena, 59, Western Cape, South Africa

"My name is Zarina - single mother of two beautiful kids. I have recently been separated from my husband & have applied for a divorce. The only thing that has kept me sane & prevented me from breaking down was the support of my family & your inspiring quotes. These were especially a life saver. I found so much comfort in it & for that I would like to thank you from the bottom of my heart. You once had a pic that says 'HOPE is the bridge between letting go & starting over on the other side.' I have it saved as my wallpaper on my phone, just so that I can always be reminded that there is hope of finding happiness again. Thank you so much once again for all your inspiring & motivational thoughts."

Zarina, Johannesburg, South Africa

"I shared most of your wonderful and beautiful quotes on Facebook and most of my friends liked and shared them. They sure inspired them, made them feel good. We find it difficult to express many delicate feelings in our routine conversations. Posts like these make it easy and enjoyable. Thanks for all of them."

Lalita, 57, India

"Hi, Judy. I will be delighted for you to use some of the details of how I share your inspirational messages with clients. I am a Nutrition and Well-being Specialist working in the UK on the beautiful Isle of Anglesey in North Wales. With the worldwide economic and financial situation, fewer jobs, obesity problem and a high proportion of stress and mental health problems, trying to encourage people to adopt more 'healthful' attitudes is pretty challenging.

For many of my clients, I have now set up an e-mail or cellphone text service and 3 or 4 times a week, I text or email them with either an encouraging message, an affirmation for them to use, or inspirational quotes from famous people. My client range is wide, from children through to the elderly so their issues are as varied as the age/social environment spread and as a private therapist I pride myself on offering a 'client specific' service. However, the wonderful encouraging words and photos used in your daily emotional wellness messages appeal to all and though one message may not have huge relevance to all on one particular day, there is bound to be someone for whom that daily message and encouragement just hits the spot."

Jan Walker, Consultant Nutritionist and Well-being Specialist at
Natural Manna, www.naturalmanna.co.uk

"The second thing in the morning (after scripture reading and prayer) that I do is check in with my online friends, and look for positive and inspirational things to share with family and friends. They (often) say thanks. It may be the positive start to their day."

Janet, USA

"What I like is that I tend to go on Facebook when I am bored and it really helps me to focus in the right direction by having sites like yours in my newsfeed. So it is the reinforcement I need at the time I need it."

Cheri, 45, Germany

"I look for your Quotes every day. You have helped me through my hardest times!! And I thank you for that. I will try to pick a favorite but there are just so many, and I have so many sites now because of you. Thank you."

Christine, 52, New York

"I write a lot of things, Judy, I just never shared them with anyone. I am only now feeling the trigger to respond because of what you write. So thank you very much. I was a recluse for a few years because of something that happened to me, so I would hide in my home after work and I just lived in my own head. I found out a lot about people and emotions of myself and others by just observing. My balcony overlooks the ocean, where I see thousands of people. I may not be able to hear what they say, but their emotions as they interact are loud. P.S. I'm not a recluse anymore!"

Irmgard, 58, Florida

TIP #111

A Behind the Scenes
"Focus on Facebook"

For this TIP, I thought it might be interesting to see some sample posts from really popular Inspirational Facebook sites, and to learn the stories and rationale behind a few sites in the wellness/personal development space. Their sites represent the positive message and creative posts that many sites in the wellness space share, and I listed some of my other favorites below after their showcasing a few of my favorites.

INSPIRATIONAL SITES SAMPLER

Patricia Love
Life's Cheerleader
Washington
facebook.com/LifesCheerleader

Why did I start my Page…Well I would have to say 60 plus years of living…!!! On the outside most would say I have had a charmed life…but little do most of them know…that I have been through Rape (cheating death) physical and mental abuse…sexual harassment, divorces, caring for an elderly mother, death of a sibling and the death of parents. Living high on the hog and drinking champagne on yachts, to searching for change in old purses for dinner…and those are just some of the highlights!! Yet somehow through every high and low…I found something within me to stay strong and to not allow people or life to bring me down….so in finding my inner cheerleader…I wanted to turn around and helps others find theirs…The response from my page has been incredible…the private messages that I get saying that I have helped my fans through major struggles and life's challenges….cheer my heart on….

Karen Hackel
The Whisper of Your Soul
New Jersey
facebook.com/thewhisperofyoursoul

The Whisper of Your Soul Facebook page was started to promote the book of the same name. Fans of the page appreciate the inspirational and spiritual posts about living life to the fullest and always remembering to listen to their inner voices.

Rebecca Terry Rahn
Never Give Up on Yourself
Kentucky
facebook.com/pages/Never-Give-Up-on-Yourself

"Who I am and why this page was started...

I have been married twice; first husband chose to end our 7-year marriage abruptly. I was a lonely single mother for 10 years hoping to find someone to trust with my heart. I am sure there are plenty of others out there who know what I'm talking about. You lose trust and it's hard to trust again.

In 2005 I met and married my second husband. We were married 4-years and had a child together. He was affected by the sluggish economy, lost his job, couldn't pay the bills or find another job. He became deeply depressed and kept slipping downhill. Unfortunately, no one could have changed the outcome because we didn't know what was about to happen. My husband committed suicide on Oct. 22nd, 2009. That was the worst day of my life; all I can remember was driving up our long driveway and seeing police cars all around. That day I felt like I was living in a CSI show.

The hardest thing I had to do was bury my husband. It never seemed real. My heart broke when our 3-year old would cry for him. There isn't a day that goes by that I don't think of him. I have my good days and my bad days...

This page was started because of the pain and depression I suffered through. I hope the positive motivation posted here can help others..."

"Some personal messages of encouragement that means the world to me 'cause I never realized that I still need so much myself. I am not sure if you knew all this Judy but this page has really helped me as much as it was designed to help others."

Kathryn Yarborough
Flowing With Change
Maryland
facebook.com/FlowingWithChange

"The social media I use the most is Facebook. On my Facebook business page, I meet new people; get to know them, and invite them to my website, and to join my e-list. To do this, I post article links to my website and information about my free e-book that they can get by joining my e-list.

I'm a certified dance/movement therapist and an integrative breathworker, my work has evolved over the years to include a focus on helping heart-based entrepreneurs do the work they're called to do via manifestation coaching.

I started offering manifestation coaching in 2005. It's a kind of alternative business coaching. In early 2012, I created Flowing with Change - an online membership community that has two "circles." The inner circle is made up of professional members - heart-based entrepreneurs who want to grow their businesses - and the outer circle includes anyone interested in personal growth and transformation. My intention, through my Facebook page is to attract people interested in personal growth to the teleconferences and other events we offer so that they can meet the Flowing with Change professional members and find out about their services. It's a win-win for everybody!"

Fiona Childs
The Positivity Toolbox
North Carolina

"Why Did I Create a Page All About Positivity Tools?–Because Positivity is powerful. It can change things!

Shortly into my career as an attorney I was blessed with my first baby girl and changed careers to work with my then-doctor-husband, operating a medical clinic. While I did find it difficult to work with people with health problems, just as I have found it difficult to work with people with legal problems, in my new work, I could let my creativity flow as I was in charge of just about everything, but the doctoring. I enjoyed that aspect of it and I was able to have a balance between mothering and working.

It was shortly after the birth of my second baby girl that my dear best friend was brutally murdered in her home one Fall night. During the weeks, months and years after she died I felt the world was turned upside down. Everything I thought was the truth seemed to no longer be; uncertainty and confusion ruled and my mind constantly raced with so many "why" questions. Michelle's death and the awful nature of it filled my every thought.

The blessing for me personally is that during that time that I was able to reflect on my own life and see that I had not been living it in a way where I was true to my own values and beliefs. I wanted more. I wanted to feel happy–like the real kind of happy that I now refer to as "joy"–the kind that is there every day and that cannot be drowned by a bad situation. This self-reflection gave me the courage to end a marriage with a man I was not compatible with and so also began my journey into a new career.

Not too long ago, after four and a half years the trial began of Michelle's killer, who was her husband at the time of her death. I sat in the trial each day over the course of almost a month. During this time I was brought to a place of utter sadness. Listening to witness after witness was agonizing. During the evenings, I sought respite in something positive to work on to take my mind away from the days. That is when the Positivity Toolbox Facebook Page was spawned.

Having become a positive-minded woman after a long period of sadness after Michelle's death, I felt I had much to contribute to a positive forum, such as Positivity Toolbox, and felt confident as the creator of such a place. I was overwhelmed (in a positive way) to watch the page grow so quickly; one night, by 1000 people! It kept me going during the time of the trial. It was my sanctuary and port in the storm. I never mentioned the trial on here (til now when I wrote this "About" section), but found immense encouragement during that time in the words of the fans who posted there. Little did they know the positive impact they were having on me and how they helped me get thru that difficult time? I truly hope that I am giving back to all the fans what they have given me!"

"I receive daily comments on my page about how much my page helps them. I also get personal messages through the page daily from people saying the same. This is so important to me and makes the page that much more special to know that I am making a contribution to other people's lives."

Doe Zantamata
Happiness In Your Life
Florida
facebook.com/Happinessinyourlife

In 2.5 years, Happiness in Your Life on Facebook grew to over 360,000 people who have found their way there for unique, daily inspiration. The goal of Happiness in Your Life is to be a catalyst for people to rethink limitations and become empowered to change any aspects of their lives that are preventing their happiness.

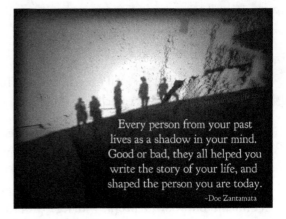

Every person from your past lives as a shadow in your mind. Good or bad, they all helped you write the story of your life, and shaped the person you are today.

~Doe Zantamata

Other Great Inspirational Sites on Facebook

Peace of the Beach: facebook.com/MariannesPeaceoftheBeach

The Dog Buddha: facebook.com/TheDogBuddha

Bedeempled Brain: facebook.com/BedeempledBrain

Be Yourself: facebook.com/beyourself09

Joy of Dad: facebook.com/joyofdad

Joy of Mom: facebook.com/joyofmom

Life Tastes Well: facebook.com/lifetasteswell

Living on the inside: facebook.com/pages/Living-on-the-inside/263707323701283

Loving Them Quotes: facebook.com/OldSchoolGranny

McMotivator: facebook.com/McMotivator

My Favorite Quotes: facebook.com/czeth0416

Quotes & Thoughts: facebook.com/quotedthoughts

Quotes Mantra: facebook.com/quotesmantras

Read, Love and Learn: facebook.com/readloveandlearn

Smiles and Rainbows: Positive Ways with Patricia Love: facebook.com/positivewayswithpatricia

Sobriety House, Inc.: facebook.com/SobrietyHouse

Soul On Fire: facebook.com/pages/Soul-On-Fire/463798670300021

SUCCESS365: facebook.com/URSUCCESS365

The Road to ME: facebook.com/pages/The-road-to-ME/256051284513570

Whisper of the Heart: facebook.com/mywhisperoftheheart

You ARE Enough: facebook.com/KnowYouAreEnough

Your Beautiful Life: facebook.com/Yourbeautifullife

TIP #112

Who Gives a Tweet?

THEORY: Twitter (twitter.com) helps promote positive messages and resources by using up to 140 characters, known as "tweets," to display a message or link to a post or any social media site. The "tweets" are short and to the point, saying a simple thought, question, or comment that helps therapists pass along a thought or announce news to their followers without making direct contact. If you read a blog post there are usually links to various social media sites to show support and share it with your "followers," and Twitter is perfect for that. By the click of the bird icon, representing Twitter, you share your message to all the people who are "following" you! It used to be that you never wanted strangers to follow you–now, the more the better!

IMPLEMENTATION: Being a rather insight-oriented person, Twitter seemed very superficial to me at first. However, I realized the power of being limited to a small number of words to express ideas succinctly and now love using Twitter to direct traffic to a recent blog post, quote or article from either myself or others that I come across in my reading. It's a quick way to share resources. I also tweet other peoples' posts that I like, and thus have built, through Twitter, a network of people who enjoy sharing resources, like blog post links.

If you like using Twitter to deliver pictures rather than words, Twitpic is a great free service to convert your pictorial inspirational quotes or blog posts into a short URL–you can tweet with a picture!

Some therapists with a Twitter interest tweet a healthy thought, link to a blog post, or a positive affirmation every day. Not near the computer enough but want to have some tweets scheduled when you are away? You can schedule tweets to post through free services like Tweetdeck (tweetdeck.com) and Hootsuite (hootsuite.com).

Don't know what to tweet? Read the tweets of others and anything that sounds good you can "retweet" and it is sent out to your followers.

There are a lot of things to know about Twitter if you use it as a tool to promote yourself and your message, but these pointers above give you a starting point if you are not a tweeter already!

PROCESSING: Twitter offers a new dimension to communication that directs people to your sites, and also offers a way to send a quick mental health message or link to promote your message of wellness! It's a great way to keep connected with your followers in a couple minutes or less!

TIP #113

Pinterest for Promoting Mental Health and Wellness in Full Color!

THEORY: Pinterest (Pinterest.com) is visual social media–it's all about pictures! Anything with a picture attached is fair game on Pinterest. As long as you have a picture attached to a quote, a blog post, an article, book, a thought, etc., it belongs on Pinterest. It is a great way to connect with other mental health professionals and people interested in self-improvement. Pinterest allows you to highlight your practice materials, mental health resources, and links to other influential books and resources, in a way that is user-friendly and can promote your platform of expertise in a fun and colorful way.

Pinterest is a series of "boards" and pictorial links with different themes of your choice. When you start a free account, you will find Pinterest is very user-friendly.

Pinterest has become a very successful marketing tool for those with products to sell, such as books, ebooks and other mental health products. Aside from the sales and marketing utility, it is a great way to share your blog posts, inspirational posts and quotes, and the increasingly popular Instagrams which are photos all put together to make a sequence. These are great for visual directions, explanations and marketing a brand showing different aspects of your product. Pinterest is fun, colorful and beautiful and is a fun way to increase your areas of expertise as well as your visibility in the public arena.

With the increasing popularity on Pinterest, there are many social media interfaces popping up that connect your social media sites like Facebook to Pinterest. My favorite is Pinvolve. Pinterest also has the ability to supply you with analytics like Google does for your site traffic, as long as your Pinterest board is verified (found under settings).

IMPLEMENTATION: I have found Pinterest to be a lot of fun, as well as informative about what other people are doing in the mental health field. I have enjoyed looking at other clinicians' handouts, worksheets, and blog posts. When I read a blog post or see a mental health site I enjoy and there is a link to Pinterest, I like to look and maybe *follow* the topics (or boards) that interest me. If I like some of their pictures, or "pins" as they call them on Pinterest, it is very easy to "re-pin" and put those posts I like onto one of my boards of the same topic. You can have as many boards as you want, each with its own content heading, and as many pictures as you want on each board. These pictures can be your material or those from others that you got from Pinterest or other websites.

Many people use Pinterest for personal reasons, and have many personal interests on their site such as recipes, beaches, favorite colors, family pictures, fashion, rainbows, cars, etc. Since I am keeping my Pinterest strictly a professional page to go with my *brand,* most of the shared community boards I join are relevant to the topics of *mental health, personal development, inspiration* and *wellness.* For example, I have a different board for each topic including self-help books, blog posts, pictorial inspirations (I call this Daily Positive Inspirations), videos for self-improvement, professional speaking topics for businesses as well as mental health professionals, other favorite personal development blogs, self-help worksheets and handouts, and more. I am also part of some community boards that I will explain in the next paragraph. I love the simple beauty of Pinterest because it allows me to put all my mental health topics, products, interests and speaking topics in the same place. It is a "clearinghouse" of my expertise and my accomplishments in the field, along with my favorite resources from the field of mental health and wellness. Think of having a pictorial view of your interests and experience, and having a fun way to showcase each topic! It is a great way to organize your work, professional interests and valuable resources under one *roof* (i.e., set of boards).

The greatest single TIP I have for getting Pinterest followers is to ask to join some community posting boards. When I was invited into a community board on which hundreds of people were given the rights by the board originator to pin on that board, I did not realize the power of having these boards. When there are a lot of people given permission by the board administrator to "pin," the boards generally have thousands of followers. Thus, when you pin your own post or *repin* someone else's post, your pin is seen by many people who you would not reach otherwise, and a portion of those people end up following you personally. It is really like free advertisement when you are on these community group boards! This became similar to the strategy I found with guest blogging–attach yourself to high profile sites in your field and then if you have good content, you get a lot of connections.

The community mental health boards and inspirational boards I am a member of are worth mentioning. To start, you might want to follow them to familiarize yourself with their mission and postings to get yourself some great information. If you are already set up with Pinterest and have mental health and personal development boards, you can ask to be a guest *pinner.*

Here is a sample of the personal development and mental health community boards that I follow or belong to:

Pinterest.com/healthyplace/mental-health-experiences

Pinterest.com/rebeccadoe/positive-words

Pinterest.com/quotedthoughts

Pinterest.com/healthyplace

PROCESSING: Pinterest has a lot of potential for personal as well as professional interests, and by having at least a foundation of the basics, now you can have fun going into what I think of as a *picture wonderland* and feel inspired and also learn from the wealth of resources you can find there.

TIP #114

LinkedIn: A Great Place for Therapists to Connect!

THEORY: LinkedIn is a wonderful social media forum for those in the mental health field, as it is a largely professional site where professionals connect with one another and share resources and even opportunities. I love being joined with groups that are in my geographical location, and also love being part of a worldwide community of people with the same interest in mental health, wellness, personal development and social media networking for wellness.

LinkedIn can help you keep connected with your professional network by being each other's "connections." It is not uncommon for people to get job or professional opportunities through LinkedIn. I personally have been on various radio shows through my various groups. With the many facets of LinkedIn, the basic one to remember is to create your profile with as much care as you would a resume–maybe even more since many more people have the potential to see it!

IMPLEMENTATION: LinkedIn is very user-friendly and is vast in its potential for networking. This is certainly not a "how-to guide" for LinkedIn, but I will offer just a few tips on what has worked for me. I believe the beauty of LinkedIn is connecting with people with similar professional interests, as well as potential consumers who might be interested in my speaking or books, and others who just enjoy sharing resources and developing LinkedIn friendships.

LinkedIn allows you to join up to 50 groups, including those you start yourself.

I personally was interested in connecting with others who had a similar focus on mental health and wellness as well as personal development, so that we could share resources, so I started a group myself called "Personal Development, Wellness and Self-Improvement Network." I have been reading peoples' blog posts and viewing their websites and have enjoyed reciprocating resources. It has been a great learning community, as are many other groups I have joined.

A small sample of the many LinkedIn mental health groups that are my personal favorites are:

Tips and Tools for Your Therapeutic and Wellness Toolbox: *This is the group that I started in order to share Tips and Tools with other practitioners inspired by the writing of this book, with the purpose of getting material for my next one–so, of course, it is one of my favorites!*

    Links for Shrinks–For Therapists, Psychologists, Coaches

    United States Mental Health Professionals

    American Counseling Association

    Psychologists, Coaches, Psychotherapists and Counselors

    Positive Thinkers

    Personal Development, Wellness and Self-Improvement Network: *Another group that I started*

PROCESSING: LinkedIn provides a powerful web-based resource for meeting your professional needs. There are so many ways that LinkedIn can be helpful to you personally and professionally. By joining groups, involving yourself in discussions, and reading some of the links that interest you, you might find that your own mental health is increased by being exposed to great people and great ideas, in a great forum!

TIP #115

A Sampling of Tips and Tools From Other Therapist's Toolboxes!

One of the best things about LinkedIn is that professionals can learn from one another. LinkedIn has been a great resource for me to discover what strategies other mental health professionals find are most useful in dealing with their clients. Just being able to do an informal survey on questions that are important to me has been very helpful–I have a "ready-made" population of therapists that I can always go to for sharing ideas and resources.

The following quotes are from various wellness and mental health professionals in some various LinkedIn groups that answered questions like, *"What is your best therapeutic tip?"* This is a sample of the responses I have gotten back (printed here with permission of the authors). If you would like your tip to be included in my next book in this series, please email your tip to: judy@belmontwellness.com

Thanks to all of the mental health and wellness professionals that responded to my inquiries on LinkedIn!

QUESTION: "What is your best therapeutic tip?"

"There is one simple but sometimes difficult yet vital task I give to many of my clients–to keep a gratitude journal. My instructions are less demanding than most gratitude journals–to write down three things each week that you are grateful for. Try to name different things but if you can't come up with any it is fine to name the same things you felt grateful for last week if you still feel that same sense of gratitude. It is an attempt at shifting the focus from the negative and what is missing and the pain to what positives may still remain within reach."

Donna Trainor, LCSW, New York

****

"I ask my clients who might be struggling with anxiety issues to put a small piece of paper on their refrigerator (or wherever they are likely to see it daily). On the paper, I ask them to simply write, "Oh, well." I think that if we all repeated this little mantra on a daily basis, it will come to mind more easily when we are stuck in traffic, or late for a meeting, or have passed a deadline at work, or forgot someone's birthday, or forgot to take out the trash, etc. Simple, but useful."

Eileen Watters, M.Ed., Mental Health Counselor/Consultant, Columbus, Ohio

****

"I would say that the best thing that I have learned in practice is: Meet a client where they are. I learned the hard way that pushing clients to be where I want them to be will only end badly. After 10 years of practice, I am able to take pause and step back to see if I am serving the client's goals or my own. Meeting the client where they are is the only way to get them to where they want (or need) to be."

Sara Quincer, MA, LCPC, www.kmadoctors.com, Sycamore, IL

****

"Let every treating doc/physician/psychiatrist/surgeon, etc. put oneself into the shoes of the prospective patients and treat them with utmost compassion and best of medical knowledge/expertise, without much bothering about the insurance/medico-legal claims/constraints/vulnerabilities."

Devinder Bawa, Family Physician at Bawa Clinic, Ludhiana Area, India

****

"I think that one of the most important tools that has helped me during periods of transition or change, times of fear and doubt, is to live 'as if.' When I recognize that my thoughts are not being supportive of my dreams and goals, I remind myself to live 'as if.' I ask myself how I would feel and behave if I had already met my goal. Instantly, and I mean instantly, my shoulders go back and my head gets higher. I feel better about myself. I notice my inner thoughts change from ones of self-doubt and fear to ones of empowerment and determination. Living 'as if' has become 'living' period."

Christina M. McCalla, www.cmccalla.com, California

****

"At times, therapy can become extremely intense and excessively focused on core pain issues, a diagnosis, a refractory and unmanageable condition, a constant focus on what's wrong, what's not working, why are things not moving, and/or why are things moving in the wrong direction. Too many issues can flood or bog a client down and imbalance other life pursuits beyond therapy. Given this, I may sometimes introduce the Life Balance Wheel.

The Life Balance Wheel (see here for one example: http://www.mindtools.com/pages/article/newHTE_93.htm) is designed to identify areas of life (spirituality, marriage, career, money, health, family, friends, being a father/mother, etc.) important to the client but often missed in therapy. The Wheel is excellent for focusing the client on positive, meaningful life actions and beliefs/values, which therapy can often miss due to its focus on 'pathology.'"

David O. Saenz, Ph.D., Ed.M., LLC, www.psych-consulting.com, Pennsylvania

****

"On Self Care I use visualization (what would I choose as a symbol of myself), and then ask the client what thoughts, feelings, actions/behaviors they would use to nurture that symbol. I list all that they tell me and then give them a copy. Recently, a client said that the first thoughts/actions they would have about their "symbol-self" was to admire it and handle delicately! They volunteered to reveal the symbol - a butterfly."

Terrance Trites, Family Therapist, Faces of Hope Family Therapy Centre, Moncton, New Brunswick, Canada

****

"I wrote my Master's research paper on this topic - "Metaphors: A Key Ingredient in Equine Assisted Psychotherapy?" I am an EAGALA certified equine assisted therapist using my horses as therapeutic tools with clients. Turns out they serve as great metaphors for issues in their lives."

Liz Letson, MS, Youth & Family Counselor, EAGALA Certified, Equine Assisted Therapist, www.eaglevistaranch.com, Minnesota

****

"I would be exploring the pay-offs for sickness and the benefits to health and the things that they currently do to keep sickness in place and health at bay.

And another thought…Pay yourself some attention. Often the pain we feel is the body's attempt to get us to 'wake up' to the reality - to the fact that, for example, when we eat certain foods our body has to work harder than with other foods. Headaches can mean insufficient water, but they can also mean that there is a situation we are not paying attention to in our lives, and it is the body's best way of getting us to 'wake up' to reality and make the external changes. Of course once the issue is addressed there is no more need for the headache so it miraculously disappears. If you can't relate to this, think of the child with the 'sore tummy' prior to school. Finding out what is going on at school may be more significant than taking them to the doctor in terms of assisting them to be healthy."

Issy Crocker, Issy Crocker and Team Limited, http://www.issycrocker.co.uk

****

"Every experience is a learning opportunity… some lessons are really hard to learn but if we don't learn from a bad time or situation we are going to face that challenge again in a different format. So it is best to take each situation and look at what it is trying to teach us so we can honor it and move on. This and more in my book- Healing What's Eating You. *Aloha and blessings."*

Keala Vai Noel, Director at Aloha Healing Women, Hawaiian Islands,
Author of *Healing What's Eating You*

****

"Spend 20 minutes a day touching base with yourself. This can be done either first thing in the morning or last thing at night or for a bonus done both times. Being still and tapping into our inner source everyday provides us with a space of calm away from our busy lives. This can be achieved either through daily meditation, yoga, or just sitting still with yourself."

Jo Inoniyegha, Inspirational Leader, Facilitator, InTuition Entrepreneur,
Hypnocoach, United Kingdom

****

"Why is it some people just naturally love to exercise and others drag through it? What if I could help you become the person who likes being active?

Wouldn't that be a blessing: instead of applying willpower, just do what comes naturally.

By reaching your feelings we can influence desires. Turn off the phone and other machines and sit or recline in a place where you're not disturbed. Set a timer for 5 minutes.

1) Close your eyes and take a deep breath and when you exhale see, in your mind's eye your breath evaporated as a mist in the air, evaporating all your attention with it.

2) Take a few more of these deep breaths.

3) Imagine back to a time of enjoyment…What did your surroundings look like?… Any special scents?…Or sounds?

4) Put your thumb and forefinger together as you indulge your senses.

5) Being in motion gives you that happy feeling. You like being in motion. Whether it's walking or dancing or even simple stretches at your desk.

6) When the timer buzzes you open your eyes feeling refreshed."

Kelly Donavan, www.Troubledtalktotyler.com, California

****

"If you have a section related to "getting stuck" there's a little trick I use. Sometimes we all get settled in and ready for a session and I find it rather humorous that we always assume the same position, the same chair, etc. So, when things seem to get bogged down, I will ask the client to change chairs, maybe even sit in my desk chair - to get a change of perspective. Sometimes it can really loosen things up and open things up to allow for a change to happen!"

Peg Truax, MA, LPC, Therapist at Stellrecht and Associates, President-Elect
Minnesota Counseling Association, Minnesota

****

"I always use the story - The Red Tree *by Shaun Tan as a stimulus for mental health education and resilience. I couple it with a visible thinking routine CSI which asks students to associate a color, symbol and image with the story. (Visible thinking is from the Harvard graduate school of education.)"*

Melissa Boyd, Head of PDHPE at Pymble Ladies' College, Sydney Area, Australia

TIP #116

Avoid Social Media Addiction: How to Stay Focused Amidst the Buzz!

Social media can become a world of its own. I have heard the term "Social Media Addiction," and it being likened to "crack" due to its addictive capabilities. It has been called iDisorder! Here are some thoughts and points to keep in mind in order to stay productive amidst the buzzzzzz.

Are you in control of your social media or is it controlling you? Are you constantly distracted from your work by the alerting sounds of tweets, dings and rings, not to mention a burgeoning number of inbox messages that just can't wait to be read? Do you have a hard time tolerating the suspense of whether or not you got new followers, new messages, new mentions— *and you just have to check?* Are you feeling increasingly anxious over not having enough time in the day to keep up with Facebook, Twitter, Twellow, WordPress, Pinterest…need I say more? Can you Digg it? Are you headed for the new mental disorder of the Social Media Age called "iDisorder"?

If these questions ring a bell, ding, tweet, or otherwise, then you might be suffering from some form of social media addiction—or at least—obsession! Before you search online for a Social Media Anonymous group, here are some essential tips to help you curb your social media addiction and stay focused amidst the buzz!

First Tip: Forgive your parents. Your parents warned you to watch out for people who followed you. They had no clue that at some point in your life, the more followers—the better! There is no way they could have imagined that you would end up going to great lengths to figure out how to attract more followers, rather than get rid of the ones you already had! As they groomed you for success, they also could not have imagined that your life success and productivity could be undermined by a quest to "like" and be "liked," never mind a chirp here and a tag there. They tried their best to instill self-esteem in you so you would think you were special no matter how many people liked you! Even watching the Jetsons™ did not provide them with any clue! So, along with the other stuff you might need the help of a therapist to forgive your parents for, forgive them for not providing you the tools to prevent social media obsession.

Second Tip: Remember that Silence is Golden! Procrastination undermines productivity, and the constant tweets and pings lure you away from focusing on your work. Even if you were not much of a procrastinator to begin with, it is just too much fun checking on your latest "likes" and "friends" or who commented on your latest discussion thread on LinkedIn. To limit the lure of all these enticements, turn off the sound on your computer, and silence the alerts on your cell phone! Turn off the instant messenger!

Better yet, if you have work to do that does not require you to be online, get offline and give it a rest! Remind yourself there are many healthier sounds to hum along with. Choose background music that can inspire, soothe and motivate you to stay on the task at hand, rather than be distracted by sound effects that only serve to lure you away! As you shut off your alerts, close down programs and take your email accounts offline, your chunks of productive time can increase significantly. If you want to set alerts to occasionally take breaks but your sounds are shut off, just use an old fashioned alarm clock or kitchen timer!

Third Tip: Silence your inner buzz! Social media is a procrastinator's friend. Amidst the buzz, you might not realize that underlying procrastination is perfectionism. People who are perfectionists are full of negative self-talk that nags at their confidence. Perfectionism tells you that you need "to be" the best rather than simply "doing" your best. Procrastination due to perfectionism makes the stakes too high to prove how good you are, and it makes it hard to be efficient and productive. So beware of the buzz of your own negative self-talk! To complicate matters, there are just so many old friends and classmates on Facebook that were not even as smart as you, and it is hard not to be distracted about their stellar accomplishments! Even if you never saw yourself as competitive, this can be very distracting when your need for approval from your work boss as well as your inner boss undermines your confidence and focus. Comparing yourself to others, anyway, is a recipe for low self-esteem, and now with Facebook, you have a new world of others to measure yourself against!

Why don't you just be yourself, since everyone else is taken?

Fourth Tip: Set limits on the time you spend with Social Media. The best way to cure obsessions and addictions is to give yourself some structure so you can "break the habit." Self-discipline is not a dirty word–it can truly set you free if you prioritize your goals and "to do" list. If you make a choice to be disciplined rather than being caught up in "have tos," you will feel less like a rebellious teenager protesting authority. If you view the ability to set limits on your time as offering a new freedom that can help you clear your head and set balanced priorities, you will learn to set better limits on your time and energy. The key to setting limits with your Social Media is to use tools that streamline your time rather than create more work for yourself. There are many apps that are designed for helping you become more organized and productive, like Buffer and Evernote.

Fifth Tip: Remember "Grandma's Rule." As you develop new habits with or without an app, keep in mind that rewarding yourself with a Facebook fix on breaks might be just the motivation you need to stay on target. Grandma's rule reminds you to reward yourself after the work is done. "First you do the work, and then you do the play." Rather than always being in the background, email, Facebook, Twitter and the like can be used as rewards for a job well done and help you stay on track. Using your social media as a reward rather than as an ongoing distraction will help you stay sane and efficient.

Sixth Tip: Unplug! Let yourself enjoy the simple pleasures in life. Take breaks without your phone, iPad or laptop. When you do, you will be recharged and then more productive in your work and in your life. It might sound counterproductive, but quality time unplugged and away will give you more energy to be productive when you are refreshed. Go outside! Learn to play again! Do something artistic! Find ways to laugh, do something with your hands, ask a friend out for lunch and leave your phone in the car or at home.

Seventh Tip: Work to Live! Part of being productive is to make sure that you are working to live, not living to work. As you bring down the distractions of social media from a buzz to a hum, you will be more in tune with what life has to offer, plugged and unplugged! Taking time to rejuvenate will make you a more focused and productive person with a healthier perspective. By getting out of the virtual world and into the "real world"–without getting beeped, tweeted, dinged or alerted–you can recalibrate yourself much like a GPS that recalibrates when you go off track. Readjust and redirect so that you will have not only a more productive life, but a happier and more balanced life too! *After all, at the end of your life, are you really going to be asking yourself, "If only I had tweeted more"?*

So what are you waiting for? Stop reading this and take a break outdoors!

(This is excerpted from one of my guest posts on www.LifeHack.org.)

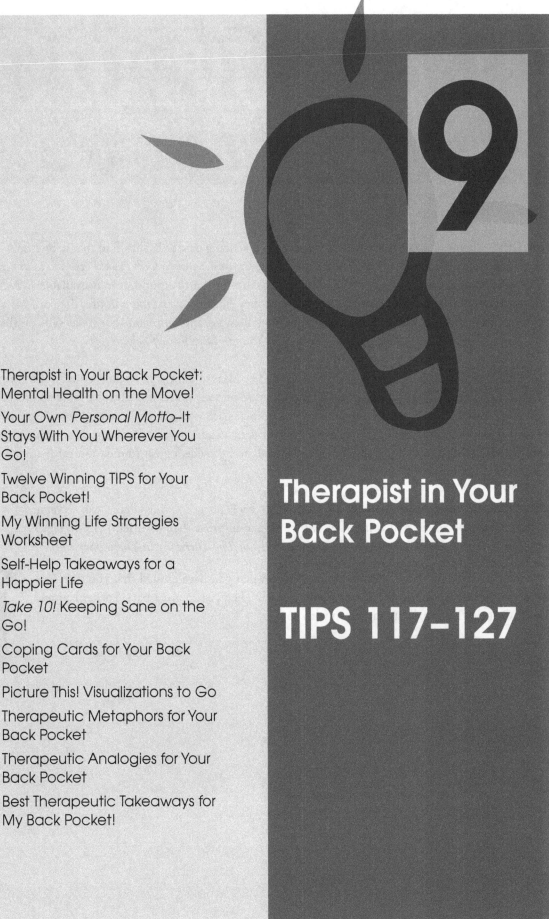

Therapist in Your Back Pocket

TIPS 117–127

TIP #117

Therapist in Your Back Pocket: Mental Health on the Move!

THEORY: Clients often feel empowered in a session practicing new skills, but find that taking those skills to the outside world is not easy. Many times I have heard my clients say things like *"I wish I could take you with me!"* This *Therapist in Your Back Pocket* section offers clients handy tips that they can carry around, readily available! Whether it be note cards, metaphorical objects, coping cards, or insights that they can find everywhere in life, they can basically have some *take out* tips and strategies to keep them on the right track between appointments. For today's life on the move, these handy *take out* tips and tools will follow them everywhere! You might call it *self-help to go!*

IMPLEMENTATION: The following TIPS are just a few ideas to offer your client mental health tips, skill reminders and activities that are very relevant to everyday life. Because of their portability and relevance to everyday life, your clients will keep mental health strategy reminders right in their back pockets! Using metaphors in everyday life can be quite powerful and help to make memorable points with your *visual learners!* Of course, using these tips and tools in your individual or group session will also be quite helpful, and provide a great foundation for helping your client use these ideas when they are *on the move!*

PROCESSING: As a result of these TIPS for their back pockets, your clients will develop insights and tools to last a lifetime. They will be able to improve their own self-help strategies and can have them available everywhere with the help of *The Therapist in Their Back Pocket!*

Are there articles, handouts, posts or other activities that you have created that you can share with your clients so that you can contribute to their Therapist in Your Back Pocket tips and tools? Or help them make up their own with you!

TIP #118

Your Own Personal Motto–It Stays With You Wherever You Go!

What is your personal motto?

What do you stand for?

What are your values?

Is there a saying that you can refer to or repeat throughout the day that can help keep you grounded and focused on your own personal mission and life goals? Do you have your own personal motto that summarizes, in a phrase, your mission and priorities? If you keep on repeating your own *personal motto*, especially in challenging situations, you will be more likely to keep *on track* with your own personal *mental health mission.* By repeating it, much like a mantra often used in meditation practice, it can guide you to a happier life!

Example: In the first chapter, I shared a couple handouts and worksheets on the concept of improving yourself rather than proving yourself. Since I provided the foundation and explanation, I am using it as a quick example for this TIP In essence, a common trap that people get caught in when dealing with friends and family is the need to prove themselves. The reason why arguments and conflict occur in relationships is that people are trying to prove how *right* they are. *So they are actually trying to prove themselves rather than improve themselves!*

For this example, a very fitting motto to help you keep on track would be:

I will not seek to *prove* myself, but rather *improve* myself!

By adopting this motto, you will stay focused on your own self-directed goals, rather than trying to prove how right you are.

Can you think of a mental health mission you would like to adopt to keep your *head on straight?*

My mission: _____

Now think of a motto!

My Motto: _____

Write your motto down, put it in your back pocket, and refer to it many times a day to be your own therapist in your back pocket!

TIP #119

Twelve Winning TIPS for Your Back Pocket!

Keep these winning TIPS in your back pocket, and refer to them throughout the day. Either use notecards for each tip and carry them all around, or take one each day. Or, bring the entire sheet and use it as a blueprint throughout your day that will give you a winning attitude everywhere you go!

1. In the game of life, accept there are some things we can't change.

Just like rolling the dice, we have no control over what comes up. We have no choice–roll with it!

2. Don't measure yourself against anyone else's yardstick.

Once you fall in the comparison trap, there will be no end to dissatisfaction.

3. Compare yourself and measure your progress only against where you have been.

Strive to improve on yesterday. You are a work in progress. Keep in mind that the most important room in the world is the room for improvement!

4. Forgive yourself for not knowing better.

Don't kick yourself in hindsight for what you did not have the ability to know in foresight. Instead of beating yourself up, use the lessons learned to redirect your life now.

5. Focus on the WHOLE, not the HOLES!

The road of life has many detours, bumps, and potholes. Make peace with the fact that progress never goes in a straight, uncomplicated line.

6. Move forward, despite occasional backward glances.

Look back only to make your life better now, not to be stuck in the land of *if onlys* and *woulda, coulda, shouldas*. Move onwards and upwards!

7. Ask for help–it helps others too!

Asking for help is a strength, not a weakness. People who do for others are also doing something special for themselves. Give them the opportunity!

8. Share the love!

After all, love is more important than anything else.

9. Enjoy your life journey.

Instead of waiting to be happy until you reach your life's goals, enjoy the scenery along the way!

10. You have nothing to prove.

Stop looking for outside recognition. Rather than *PROVE* yourself, *IMPROVE!*

11. It's not about how hard you fall, but how you get yourself back up.

Stumbles set the stage for success, if you learn from your setbacks.

12. Winners in life *Do* –they don't *Stew.*

If you are proactive, rather than reactive, you will take charge of your life.

Are you a winner in the game of life? If you learn from life's winners you will truly be a winner! Accept the cards you are dealt, and be too busy playing your hand to complain about any lousy cards.

TIP #120
My Winning Life Strategies Worksheet

Which TIPS would you like to carry around in your back pocket?

1. From TIP 119, pick the two that seemed the most relevant to you to answer the questions below. Write the tips here and then answer the following questions as to why they resonated with you.

    TIP 1: _____

    _____

    TIP 2: _____

    _____

2. Why are these TIPS challenging for you?

    TIP 1: _____

    _____

    TIP 2: _____

    _____

3. Name an action or "game plan" for each TIP that you can implement in your life.

    TIP 1: _____

    _____

    TIP 2: _____

    _____

4. Choose one negative thought associated with each of your TIPS and turn them into positive self-statements to give you an edge in the game of life!

    TIP 1: _____

    _____

    TIP 2: _____

    _____

If you keep these handy TIPS in your back pocket, surely happiness will follow you wherever you go!

1. Stop waiting for things to change–change yourself NOW!

Change your attitude and truly change your life! Many times people have preconditions to happiness, only to find even if they reach that goal, there are even more pre-conditions to happiness. Aside from a temporary "high" when we attain our goal, we very quickly go back to a general baseline mood unless we change our thinking. ***Real attitude change is an inside job!***

2. Build on your regrets, rather than letting them keep you stuck in the past.

Don't use the past as a hitching post–use it as a guidepost. What's done is done, and you can't change it now. Use lessons from the past to improve your life NOW! Even failure can be seen as feedback, not as a referendum of your self-worth. Use your regrets as stepping stones towards a better future, rather than rocks in your back pocket that weigh you down!

3. Learn something every day.

The end of school does not mean the end of learning. We are learning all the time, even if we are not aware of it. Life teaches us lessons no one ever could. If you open up to the wonder of growing and learning, even if the lessons are something you never wanted to learn, you will keep moving in a forward direction.

4. Stop lying to yourself!

People who are the most honest to others are often the biggest liars to themselves. They feed themselves all sorts of fiction that they are not good enough, not smart enough, not attractive enough, to the extent that they feel at times like *failures*. Don't keep that judgmental inner voice in your back pocket–throw it away!

5. Forgive…for goodness sake!

Forgiveness does not mean condoning behavior–it means you give up the bitterness you harbor that eats at you and robs you of happiness in life. People who wrong us are not inherently evil, but more likely unhealthy and maybe *very, very, very* unhealthy. Of course, the most important person to forgive is yourself, and keep in mind you are a work in progress.

6. Think straight to feel great!

As you become more aware of irrational patterns of thinking and change them into more rational thoughts, you will be empowered to change your attitude to change your life. *"I can't stand this"* is irrational–nothing makes you melt into the ground! A more rational perspective is, *"I am having a hard time with this"*. The less you immobilize yourself with judgmental thoughts, the more you will feel empowered and optimistic.

7. Try to change what is in your control, not what is out of your control.

Who is the only person we can change? *Ourselves!* Who do we often try to change? *Others!* Even trying to change someone else's mind, however well meaning, can lead to frustration, since people do not change just because you want them too—they need to want to! People who tend to be negative and focus on changing others rather than themselves are more likely to be dissatisfied with their lives.

8. Make peace with the fact that life is not fair.

We all know that life is not fair, but all too often we still expect it to be! Expecting that life and people in it should be fair is the source of limitless emotional pain. Life gets quite tedious when you adopt that type of entitled mentality. Try as hard as you can to make life fair, and accept the rest.

9. Let yourself smile from within.

People who are grateful for what they have tend to be happier people than those people that feel bitter about what they do not have. Gratitude will never happen unless we learn to be grateful for things in our life now, with no preconditions. Life can be tough and it is easy to find faults with it, but it will be an easier journey if we stop to smell the roses. Are you too busy for that? Let yourself be a human being instead of a human doing.

10. Don't wait for your life to change!

Tomorrow is forever put off, and today is the day to start. You can empower yourself by using "victor" language instead of "victim" language. Replace "I should" with "I will" and replace "I hate" with "I don't like." The more flexible your self-talk is, the more you will feel empowered and the more you will be proactive.

If you carry these tips around in your back pocket, and refer to them often, you will truly find that happiness will follow you everywhere!

Are there other takeaways you would add for a happier life?

TIP #122
Take 10! Keeping Sane on the Go!

Too busy in your hectic life to "take ten" to ground yourself for the day? Too much to do and too little time? Stressed out beyond belief and you can't imagine sparing any extra time to stop, take stock and take a daily pulse? Do you want to get off this endless cycle of "to dos" but can't seem to get away from your life "inbox"? Just when you feel like you cannot take "one more thing," perhaps it's time to try following this handout for at least one week to help keep you centered and focused in your busy life. These are great "take out" tips for those on the go!

Take the TAKE 10 Challenge! For one week carry this handout around in your back pocket to take ten minutes out of your busy day to spend ten minutes keeping yourself sane!

1st Minute: Start the day by writing out one positive intention.

Think of an action or resolution that will help you put a positive spin on the day.

Examples: Today I will make an effort to smile more. When I am in the meeting, I will say at least two things even if I fear sounding stupid.

2nd Minute: Take a mindfulness moment for morning mediation.

Consciously slow your breathing, taking deep breaths and attempt to focus only on the sensations around you. How do you feel? What do you smell? What do you visualize?

Example: Help yourself breathe deeply by putting your hand on your stomach, feeling it extend and deflate as you breathe. Most of us have shallow breathing and this is "backwards breathing" as they teach in yoga.

3rd Minute: Have a menu of inspirational quotes or passages on hand that you can choose from every day.

A moment of inspiration will prevent a lot of mental perspiration!

Example: "If opportunity doesn't knock, build a door." - Milton Berle "We might not have it all together, but together we have it all!" - Unknown.

4th Minute: Think in *victor* language and not *victim* language.

Take an inventory of any negative thoughts that interfere with a positive outlook and take a minute to *W.A.I.T.* and ask yourself: *What Am I Thinking?* Identify irrational, judgmental thoughts and replace them with more rational thoughts. Separate fact from fiction!

Example: Replace negative and illogical thoughts such as, "My boss made me so mad yesterday. I can't stand him" with "I was mad when my boss raised his voice to me yesterday and scolded me, and I will tell him I do not deserve to be talked to like that."

5th Minute: Each day strive to be conscious of gratefulness for the gift of life.

Identify at least three things you are especially grateful for.

Example: I am grateful that I have a family that loves me and to whom I can give love, that I have freedom to choose a positive attitude, and that I get another chance to learn from and build on my successes and mistakes of my yesterdays.

6th Minute: Surrender any grudges and bitterness.

Realize that a lack of forgiveness pulls you into the world of negativity, and strive to forgive everyone for everything.

Example: I forgive my ex-spouse for falling short in his behavior towards me and although I do not condone certain behaviors, I will not keep the bitterness within–it only poisons me.

7th Minute: Visualize a successful outcome today.

Even if it does not come true the way you visualize, the positive visualization makes your attitude more positive no matter what!

Example: Role play in your mind or visualize a calm response in dealing with your argumentative children.

8th Minute: Smile and Say Cheese!

Swiss cheese is full of holes–and so are our lives! It's how you get through these holes that counts! So smile and embrace life's imperfections! Learn and grow from them!

Example: I will make an effort to have a sense of humor when faced with obstacles instead of losing my sense of humor when things do not go the way I think they "should."

9th Minute: Stretch your mind!

Think of a metaphor that will inspire you today. Comprise a list of metaphors to pick from each day. Think of your metaphor as your daily mascot to keep you in check!

Example: One powerful metaphor is that of the sunflower. A sunflower is big, bold, loves light and with enough sunlight grows rapidly and robustly. It reminds us that if we keep thinking positively, we will flourish!

10th Minute: Tell yourself something nice about yourself each day.

This is called a positive affirmation. Tell yourself something you really admire about yourself, and this reminder will help you start the day off right by *thinking straight to feel great!*

Example: I am proud that I keep trying new things and I embrace change.

Wishing you the best on taking a time out as you work on transforming your life and yourself 10 minutes at a time! Are you truly too busy for that?

TIP #123
Coping Cards for Your Back Pocket

The use of Coping Cards is a Cognitive Behavioral technique developed by Judith Beck, Ph.D. at the Beck Institute for Cognitive Therapy and Research. Coping cards are small note cards–perfect for your back pocket–that will offer you reminders throughout your day of positive thoughts that can help you cope.

For example, if you are nervous about going to a party, with coping cards you can bring some positive self-statements in your back pocket to keep you grounded. Positive coping statements in this case would be:

- I can get through this.
- My opinion of myself is much more important than what they think of me.
- I can learn from this anxiety and learn to face the fear rather than give in to it.
- Besides, it would not be the end of the world if I felt anxious and just left early.

Other coping cards might present reminders of self-soothing strategies to use under stress. For instance, the cards might have different ideas that you can do that would be relaxing, such as

- Breathe deeply and close my eyes for one minute to allow myself to be refreshed.
- Take a walk.
- Call a friend.
- Listen to music.

Other ways to use coping cards is to have a negative thought on one side and a positive alternative on the other side. This will keep you reminded that you do not have to give in to negative, self-berating messages–there is always a more positive alternative.

By carrying these coping cards with you wherever you go, in your purse or back pocket, you will be your own best friend–and your own best self-help therapist–on the go! Below are actual coping cards used by a psychotherapy client of mine who was in counseling for anxiety and low self-esteem. She laminated and color-coded the cards–the pink cards were positive affirmations, the purple cards were self-deprecating irrational thoughts and on the other side, more rational alternatives. The blue cards were her "should" cards, in which she wrote some of her unhealthy shoulds.

Here is a sample of her different coping cards:

One Side	Alternate Side
I shouldn't take things so personally.	I'll learn how not to blow it out of proportion.
I am ashamed of myself.	I am proud I am brave enough to seek help.
I feel like a failure.	I am proud that even though I grew up with no direction, I found my own.

How about making up your own coping cards?

- You can give yourself some positive affirmations to support yourself under stress.

- You can have daily reminders of the goals you are working on.

- You can write down your negative thoughts and then replace those thoughts with more positive alternatives.

- You can write down activities you can do if you are under stress to self-soothe.

- You can ask someone close to you to write words of support for you to carry around in your back pocket!

- How about a quote or affirmation-a-day to carry with you? You can make some notecards with a quote or affirmation and pick one each day out of a bag for take out!

- How about writing on your "back pocket cards" those things that you are grateful for, so that gratefulness will follow you wherever you go?

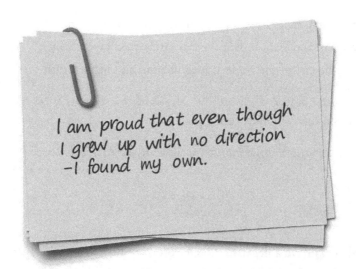

TIP #124

Picture This! Visualizations to Go

How do you picture your life?
Do you want to make a new script? Change the channel?
How about carrying a visualization around?

It can be a picture of a place that represents calmness and happiness to you.

It can be an image that captures your imagination and represents a goal you are striving towards.

It might be an image from an inspirational post you find on Facebook or the internet that helps keep you grounded and that you find soothing.

You might have many of them at home and take one a day.

As the saying goes, an inspirational visualization a day will keep the doctor away!

TIP #125

Therapeutic Metaphors for Your Back Pocket

We all use metaphors frequently in our daily lives and often don't even realize we are doing it! So often, figures of speech are metaphors and they are so well entrenched that we sometimes forget that they cannot be taken literally! For example, "painting yourself into a corner" is an expression we all know, but it is not really about using paint! Rather, we are boxing ourselves in (using another metaphor!), or better yet, we are "trapping" ourselves or making us a "prisoner" in the corner. You get the idea of how we use a "boatload" of metaphors all the time, and often do not even realize it since they are now well-accepted figures of speech! Can you think of others? Or do you want to just "cross that bridge" when you come to it?

Use metaphors to your advantage. Many times people bring around an item with them that is metaphorical and soothing for them—in a purse, wallet, and even in your back pocket! If you are having a challenging time, what metaphor would help you? What small article in your back pocket will represent something soothing and helpful as you cope with challenges? What small visual prop symbolizes strength, courage and self-acceptance?

Metaphors are so powerful because they:

- Allow us to shift our perspective and unlock old ways of thinking that do not work.
- Help us think flexibly.
- Evoke emotion, and feelings are the keys to change.
- Help us understand better than words alone, as metaphors use both words and visualizations.
- Offer us increased insight by associating a concept with an example that we understand well in everyday life.

Here are some ideas for using metaphorical items as therapeutic touchstones:

- A toy soldier reminds you to be brave and fight for what you believe in!
- A small angel would be an idea to keep in your back pocket to remind yourself that here is hope and you are not alone.
- An eraser in your back pocket reminds you that it's okay to make mistakes!
- A pencil or pen in your back pocket can remind you to write yourself a happy life now!
- A small bouncing ball can help you keep in mind that you can always bounce back!
- A marble, in case you feel like you are losing your marbles, here is a spare!
- A button to remind you that no one can push your buttons—you hold them in your back pocket!
- A dice to remind you that many things occur by chance, though we still can enjoy the game of life!
- A small sea shell to remind you of peaceful days on the beach.

- A little pearl-like object–to remind you that you hold the pearls of wisdom for your life!

- A bandage to help you heal and soothe your hurts.

- A post-it note with a note to yourself on it, to remind yourself how special you are!

- A crayon to put more color into your world!

- A balloon to remind you to "lighten up!"

TIP #126

Therapeutic Analogies for Your Back Pocket

Having analogies in your virtual back pocket is similar to having a metaphor, but it is not necessarily tangible and portable in your actual back pocket. An analogy is similar to metaphors, but it is more complicated than a metaphor, and an analogy actually might contain metaphors within it. An analogy is really a *logical argument.* My favorite analogy is the premise of my self-help book that I wrote with co-author Lora Shor, ***The Swiss Cheese Theory of Life!*** (PPM, 2011)

In this title there is an implied comparison between two seemingly different concepts, in this case *life* and *Swiss cheese.* In analogies, if two things are alike in one way, conclusions can be drawn that they are alike in other ways as well. For example, the first chapter of the book states that fondue can never turn back into a block of cheese: giving up the habit of regret. So as you can see, analogies are more complex than metaphors and might contain many metaphors, like in the case of our book. Not only do we use the image of the block of melted cheese to make a point, but we are associating this image of melted cheese with the concept of regret.

To further the analogy of Swiss and life itself, we make the point that life is not predictable like American or cream cheese. Rather, it is like Swiss with all its holes, and it's how you get through the holes that count! The analogy goes further in that the bigger the holes, the more flavorful and pungent the cheese. Just like in life, the more obstacles we overcome, the more distinctiveness and character we develop. To make the analogy even stronger, we explain that the holes in the cheese are actually called "eyes," the eyes help us develop insight and empathy. There is actually such a thing as blind Swiss, which is Swiss with no holes (like Laughing Cow cheese)–but we call that *cheese in denial!*

So next time you go by the deli counter at your grocery store, spend a moment to allow yourself to check out the holes in the Swiss, and let it remind you of an important life lesson that this TIP reveals–that life is more like Swiss than American or cream cheese, and it's how we get through the holes that counts! If we do not expect that life will go as planned, we will take things more in stride and not get as indignant when people, the weather, and life itself goes in ways we can't predict, and that might seem downright unfair!

When you go out in your everyday life, can you think of other analogies of life besides Swiss? For tennis and golf enthusiasts, I have thought many times that the games both represent so much about life itself!

This time, it's your turn to draw those analogies!

How do you think they are alike?

_____

Can you think of others?

_____

TIP #127

Best Therapeutic Takeaways for My Back Pocket!

From time to time, it helps to review some important lessons and takeaways that you have found most valuable in the course of counseling.

These questions below are designed to help you reflect on the most helpful lessons that you want to take away from your sessions with your therapist. Write them out, carry them around with you and review and revise these takeaways regularly. In essence, by crystallizing the most important takeaway lessons from your therapy sessions, it will be like having a therapist in your back pocket! These best mental health takeaways will follow you wherever you go!

1. My most important therapeutic *takeaways* that I have learned through counseling are:

_____

_____

_____

2. What are some of my favorite handouts or worksheets that I need to review periodically?

_____

_____

_____

3. How can I incorporate these TIPS into my everyday life?

_____

_____

_____

4. What support can I enlist to help me apply these TIPS, whether it is other resources or people in my life?

_____

_____

_____

5. What areas do I still need to continue to work on and what are some strategies?

_____

_____

_____

AUTHOR BIO

Judith Belmont, MS has been a psychotherapist for 35 years, with a focus on practical, psycho-social and psycho-educational skills training. She is the author of PESI's popular 3 book series, TIPS and Tools For The Therapeutic Toolbox, offering practical, action oriented strategies to help people develop healthy life skills. Judy is also co-author of the self-help book, *The Swiss Cheese Theory of Life!* Judy is a national speaker on various mental health and wellness topics for a variety of populations, including mental health professionals, women's conferences and expos, as well as workplace wellness programs.

127 MORE AMAZING TIPS & TOOLS FOR THE THERAPEUTIC TOOLBOX

CBT, DBT and Beyond

by

JUDITH BELMONT, MS

Author of

86 TIPS and Tools for the Therapeutic Toolbox

103 Groups Activities and TIPS

The Swiss Cheese Theory of Life! (co-author)

Copyright © 2013 by Judith Belmont

Published by
PESI Publishing and Media
CMI Education Institute, Inc
3839 White Ave
Eau Claire, WI 54703

Cover Design: Amy Rubenzer
Layout Design: Bookmasters + Matt Pabich
Edited By: Kayla Omtvedt

Printed in the United States of America

ISBN: 978-1-93612-843-3

PESI
Publishing
& Media
www.PESI.com